"Because it is so hard for a business to keep a secret secret, read this book. Litigation attorney Boris Parad helps you make sense of intelligence gathering in the Information Age from all the angles. Whatever the size or nature of your business, "Commercial Espionage: 79 Ways Competitors Can Get Any Business Secrets" divulges practical advice you can use every day. This straightforward primer, loaded with invaluable information and savvy suggestions, will be your secret weapon whether you want to preserve business secrets or procure them."

Michael B. Hyman, Commercial Litigation Partner with
Much Shelist Freed Denenberg Ament Bell & Rubenstein, P.C.
Chicago, IL

"If you look at novels written by lawyers in the last few years, you will find that they all present litigators at work. Grisham, Turow, Martini, and others set forth their drama in courtrooms. They seldom write about who pays the cost of the litigation. That cost is considerable. Preventing it is not all that dramatic, but it is often the best way a lawyer can serve a client. Boris Parad has told us a number of ways that business people can either prevent the loss of information to prospective pirates or anticipate the attacks of people who would purloin that information. "Commercial Espionage: 79 Ways Competitors Can Get Any Business Secrets" must be of great interest to lawyers who advise clients on ways to protect the information that is vital to their businesses. It should also be of similar value to businessmen who have information to protect. I endorse the approach that Mr. Parad has taken in outlining ways to protect information and things that others may do to steal that information."

Donald Reynolds, Director of the Intellectual Property Center at
The John Marshall Law School, Chicago, IL

COMMERCIAL ESPIONAGE:
79 WAYS
COMPETITORS CAN GET
ANY BUSINESS SECRETS

■ IN ANY COUNTRY ■

By BORIS PARAD, J.D.

Global Connection, Inc.

COMMERCIAL ESPIONAGE: 79 WAYS COMPETITORS CAN GET ANY BUSINESS SECRETS

Author: BORIS PARAD, J.D.

First Edition

Library of Congress Number: 97-094209

ISBN Number: 0-9658050-0-X

Copyright Number: TXu 701-017

Printed in the United States of America

Credits:
Editor: Joshua Kilroy
Graphic Design:
Serge Manoshin, e-mail: smanoshin@earthlink.net

Publisher:
Global Connection, Inc.
P.O. Box 688
Skokie, IL 60076-0688
Website: http://www.denvica-mall.com
E-mail address: global@denvica-mall.com

DEDICATION

This book is dedicated to the memory of my parents Samson and Sara, with all my love and gratitude for giving me everything they had and could.

ABOUT THE AUTHOR

Boris Parad, an American attorney with extensive engineering experience in Europe and the United States, is the principal in a civil litigation firm. As a patent attorney representing major U.S. corporations and numerous business enterprises, he was extensively involved with technology transfer, intellectual property protection and corporate intelligence collection matters.

Boris Parad is a member of the Association Internationale pour la Protection de la Propriete Industrielle, American Trial Lawyers Association, American Society for Industrial Security and International Association for Industrial Property Protection.

He was listed in "Who's Who in American Law" and his commercial espionage countermeausure guides for businesses have been published in Europe and the United States.

FOREWORD

Since the end of the Cold War commercial espionage has taken on a new, and increasingly important role. The global marketplace and global workplace create unparalleled opportunities for companies to gain competitive information through various shadowy methods, both legal and illegal.

Detection and enforcement of laws regarding theft of trade secrets or other valuable commercial information provide only one aspect of a well-run company's program to combat commercial espionage. That is because once a secret is out, it is out. As has been said, it is hard to put toothpaste back into the tube.

Boris Parad, J.D., has written a constructive book that provides a good outline of practical steps to prevent competitors from learning commercial secrets in the first instance. "Commercial Espionage: 79 Ways Competitors Can Get Any Business Secrets" is one of the first, and one of the clearest, explanations yet of how competitors can attack a company. It provides a blueprint showing how weaknesses can be exploited in a competitive environment. Mr. Parad, a lawyer by training, teaches any company in any country how to better defend itself against unfair commercial attacks on secret business information.

This useful book could not be more timely. The protection of secret business information is increasingly important to the competitiveness of businesses everywhere, and no more so than in America. Indeed, the economic strength of the United States is now keenly tied to its ability to protect its intellectual property. Now even foreign governments are involved in economic intelligence gathering activities. Former CIA Director William Webster said, "There is now universal recognition that economic strength is the key to global influence and power... throughout the next decade we will continue to see an increased emphasis on economic competitiveness as an intelligence issue." The Federal Bureau of Investigation now considers economic espionage to be one of the top national security threats posed by foreign intelligence operatives.

The FBI has compiled a National Critical Technologies List (NCTL). These are the companies that may especially be considered targets of intelligence activities. The list includes: advanced materials, sophisticated manufacturing technologies, information and telecommunications, biotechnology and life sciences, aeronautics and surface transportation, and energy and environmental technologies. According to the FBI, significant loss of proprietary information in these industries would not only be adverse for the companies but would undermine the U.S. strategic industrial position. Thus, there is a growing awareness across the world of the direct relationship between economic strength and national security. Today it is estimated that economic espionage in the United States alone costs U.S. businesses as much $100 billion per year.

What can companies do? The first and most important step to protecting a company's valuable business information is to understand the threat. The table of contents of this book alone provides a useful compendium of ways competitors can gain access to the corporate jewels. Using this information to form a strategic business security plan can do a great deal to ensure the preservation of competitive advantages gained the old fashioned way-by earning them.

Mark T. Banner, Patent Litigation Partner with
Banner & Witcoff, LTD. Chicago, IL

TABLE OF CONTENTS

PART 6

INTRODUCTION

You will learn 79 techniques used by the intelligence services of foreign countries and private industries for collecting proprietary business information, trade secrets and "know-how." Methods of corporate intelligence collection are of great importance to all businesses. You will see how competitors obtain other people's business secrets and understand how valuable data may be leaked out or lost.

This book details both legal and illegal methods of obtaining proprietary information. The data is drawn from published media reports, research of commercial databases, literature and case law, as well as the author's personal experience as a legal counsel. No privileged information or matters affecting national security are disclosed.

Knowledge of corporate intelligence collection techniques helps businesses to design data protection measures. Most of the information may be gathered through legal means if one knows how to do this. Sometimes the line dividing legitimate and illegitimate data collection is fuzzy. For example, employment of a manager who worked in another company may be considered an act of commercial espionage, i.e. illegal hiring away of the competitor's key employee for trade secret misappropriation. This book helps to identify legal pitfalls which can be easily avoided.

Proprietary information can be used offensively or defensively, that is to collect as well as protect business secrets regardless of the size, geographic location or type of business. The techniques succinctly described here range from cloak-and-dagger methods (theft, blackmail, mole planting, seduction, eavesdropping) to modern data accumulation measures (electronic surveillance, hiring away key employees, Internet surfing, phony business purchase negotiation, reverse engineering, fake employment interviews, etc.).

Every business has valuable data, such as customer and supplier identities; economic, technological and product research results; and sales and business plans. In view of global and local cut-throat competition, knowledge of corporate intelligence gathering techniques can help every business enterprise in acquiring or protecting data.

This book illustrates cases of business demise and devastating financial losses resulting from pilferage of corporate secrets. Most of these losses could have been avoided if the preventive measures had been developed and implemented by the victimized companies. A brief outline of such preventive measures is examined and discussed hereunder. Most of them are universally applicable to any type of business. If the techniques are not appropriate for a particular institution, they still may be adapted or modified to fit the activity of that institution.

This compendium of proprietary information collection and protection methods is critically important for any scientist, engineer or businessman in any country.

You should know how to protect your "know-how"

PART 1

INTANGIBLE COMMODITY:
PROPRIETARY INFORMATION/BUSINESS SECRETS

Information is Money

People pay doctors, lawyers, accountants, financial planners, stock brokers, economists and other experts/consultants for their advice which represents distilled technical information.

Business information is an intangible asset which can be sold, exchanged, licensed, misappropriated, and depreciated. Such information may be very simple and obtainable without any significant expense or effort. It may be acquired or lost through employees, customers, negotiations, advertising and sales literature, suppliers, theft, and so on.

Proprietary Information is a Powerful Weapon

A small company can force a giant concern to go out of business by using such tools as patent infringement or trade secret suits resulting in multimillion dollar awards. Many small companies not only suffer losses, some of them are simply destroyed by unscrupulous competitors.

Illustration:

Ellery Systems, Inc. of Boulder, Colorado, went out of business in 1994 when its Chinese competitor began to sell the communications software developed by Ellery cheaper and faster. Investigation revealed that the Chinese company had paid to a former Ellery employee $550,000 for the Ellery's software source code. This business data gave the competitor an advantage which drove Ellery out of business. Note: neither the Chinese company nor the employee were prosecuted or punished.[1]

Every Business has Valuable Proprietary Information

Proprietary business information is not limited to manufacturing concerns or technology related matters, such as "know how" of a product manufacturing process or a secret chemical formulae. Business people often do not realize the value of their proprietary information. It may consist of methods for the determination of a price for a custom-built equipment; marketing and advertising plans; work force analysis; research reports; customer lists; knowledge of tolerances in manufacturing of a multipart product; evaluation of competitor's services; and so forth.

Let us consider for a moment what secret information should be protected by a bank. Everything a bank, or a financial institution, spends its money on is an asset. Every piece of research, from investigation of personal finances to socioeconomic and political conditions in Third World countries, contains valuable proprietary information which can be sold, exchanged or otherwise used by the institution.

Misappropriation of that information can lead not only to the loss of an asset, but may even hurt the business in general. This may happen when embarrassing facts about the bank are revealed. The illegally acquired facts which may harm the bank's business include: number of bad loans; unauthorized or poorly prepared reports; incompetence or gross mistakes of employees; accounting methods; personal data of clients; research reports serving as a basis for the institution's opinions or investment decisions; merger, divestiture and acquisition reports;

and information provided by other institutions or agencies on a confidential basis.

Information Saves Money

Knowledge of better ways to design and manufacture a product gives the proprietor a competitive advantage. Stolen information saves years of research time and tremendous amounts of money.

Illustration:

A General Electric Co. employee sold computer printouts of new motor designs for $17,700 to a competing company. The competitor used this information to redesign their products and sold them cheaper than GE distributors. GE's estimate of lost business in addition to research and development costs: about $12 million.[2] Not a bad "research and development" deal: paying $17,700 for the $12 million property with no penalty, criminal or civil, levied against the aggressive competitor.

Data Misappropriation Impunity

The return on an "investment" (theft) can be phenomenal, even if the perpetrator is caught.

Illustration:

A Japanese corporation paid an employee of a U.S. company (Celanese Corporation) about $130,000 for information valued at a minimum of $6 million dollars. "Punishment" expense: the corporation's subsidiary was fined only a few hundred thousand dollars and the employee was jailed for four years.[3]

The probability of being prosecuted is reduced by the fact that many businessmen are hesitant to sue or even to acknowledge the theft of secrets. Their logic is that the damages can be compounded by the public disclosure of the stolen material and company's security measures. So it is better to cut the losses and prevent further damage to the business.

Industrial Espionage by Countries

In the post-Cold War era, beginning in 1991, most of the intelligence services have placed more emphasis on economic espionage. Each country tries to assist its domestic industries' with the results of commercial intelligence gathering while protecting domestic companies from economic pilferage by foreign agencies and companies. The U.S. government issued a classified set of intelligence priorities in 1995 and established the National Counterintelligence Center (NCC) in 1994. The purpose was to assist private industry executives in monitoring and analyzing worldwide economic espionage activities which were targeting American business enterprises. The NCC's role is to integrate and coordinate activities of the national intelligence services including the CIA, Department of Defense, FBI, Justice and State Departments, Overseas Security Advisory Commission and the National Security Council.[4]

Illustrations of Government Agency's Assistance:

(1) Newspaper reports disclosed that the CIA provided U.S. negotiators with car-trade rival's bargaining position in the U.S.- Japan trade talks.[5]

(2) The CIA also discovered a bribe offer extended to the Brazilians in order to help the French telecommunications conglomerate Thompson win a government contract. The CIA then passed that information to the U.S. company Raytheon which matched Thompson's bid and won the contract.[6]

(3) It has been reported that economic espionage techniques used by France's General Directorate for External Security, or DGSE, against U.S. companies range from planting "moles" for ascertaining business plans and electronic eavesdropping to wining and dining aerospace company executives at the Paris air show, while secretly inspecting the latest American products kept in restricted areas and photographing documents in the executives' hotel rooms.[7]

Modern data collection of technical innovations has many facets, such as purchasing knowledge by paying tuition in the university, or by reviewing technical publications, etc. All U.S. science and technology reports are monitored by scientists around the world. In South Korea, approximately 5,700 translators scrutinize U.S. technical publications. In Japan, more than 5,000 engineers and scientists review foreign technical reports. Approximately 13,000 Japanese citizens are studying in U.S. universities (about 1,000 of them major in engineering); while no more than seven U.S. students a year studied engineering in Japan during the last twenty years. More than half of the candidates for U.S. engineering Ph.D.'s are foreigners.[8]

Theft by Employees and Competitors

According to the American Society for Industrial Security survey of 325 U.S. companies, theft of proprietary information occured at an average of thirty-two (32) incidents a month and caused total losses of more than five billion dollars in 1995. A majority of the incidents (seventy four percent) were caused by insiders (people with a trusted relationship obligating people to protect information disclosed to them), such as employees, business partners, contractors, suppliers, ex-employees and retirees. The rest of the incidents were attributed to domestic competitors, foreign competitors and intelligence services, media, government and computer hackers. The leading locations for foreign incidents were in England, Canada, Germany, Japan, China and France. The most sought after items of proprietary information were long-term business and marketing plans, technological processes and research and development data.[9]

The ingenious ways of getting proprietary information are examined in the following chapter.

PART 2

CORPORATE INTELLIGENCE
COLLECTION TECHNIQUES

Economic espionage implies obtaining secret information by foreign spy agencies. The spies, using "cloak and dagger" tactics, kidnap and torture innocent victims, kill or enslave scientists, eavesdrop on secret conversations, recruit other spies and so on. These traditional ways of misappropriating information are still practiced by intelligence services. The need for using "physical" methods of extracting information has greatly diminished with the advance of technology and global data communication.

Foreign governments and spy agencies account for less than ten percent of the stolen proprietary information in the United States. Competing private companies are responsible for the majority of the pirated intellectual property.

Nowadays, almost all "secret" business information may be acquired without invoking unlawful means. The following compilation of information gathering techniques comprises legal and "not so legal" means of business intelligence (secret) collection.

1. HIRING AWAY

A key employee of a target company can be hired permanently, or temporarily as a consultant, in order to use the employee's knowledge or ability to obtain vital information.

Illustrations of trade secrets misappropriated in such a way:

(1) barbecue methods of meat cooking;[1] (2) techniques for running a smoke cessation program;[2] (3) a list of stockholders in investment companies;[3] (4) manufacturing drawings, reproduced by former employees from memory, for a hydraulic load weighing cell;[4] (5) food diet formula for rats, guinea pigs and dogs.[5]

In general, hiring employees away with the intent to gain knowledge of a particular project or product is deemed to be stealing trade secrets, even if there is no direct evidence that confidential information was extracted from such ex-employees.[6] It is rather difficult to prove such intent since employees are free to change jobs.

The employee's knowledge of doing things the right way and knowledge of "blind alleys" in product development can be legally used by the new employer. However, the disclosure of a particular design, trade secret, or specific product which became known to the employee during his employment, provides an unfair advantage to the subsequent employer.

This traditional way of getting "fresh blood" is applicable to employees on all levels of a corporate hierarchy, starting from a maintenance man to the company's president. But there could be penalties for such employee raid.

Illustration of possible consequences of a brain raid:

The New York Stock Exchange ruled that Paine Webber Group, Inc. must pay Prudential Securities, Inc. $2.5 million for hiring away four brokers and three sales assistants in 1993. This en masse brain drain (employee raid) caused substantial business losses and forced Prudential to sell its Gainesville, Florida, office.[7]

2. "EVALUATION"

Copious documentation is requested in order to "evaluate" the contemplated "purchase" of the target product or "use" of the targeted service. Even the temporary custody of a valuable item may be requested. Once that item is obtained, it is then stealthily audio, photo or video recorded for subsequent integration of the learned data into the evaluating party's or its principal's own products.

Illustration:

A company "N" needs to know how low-friction ball bearings are made. "N" uses a company "S", either well-established or newly organized, as a would-be purchaser of either the manufacturing company or its technology. Product samples, specifications, lists of suppliers and customers, equipment used for manufacturing, names of key employees, business and marketing plans, names of advertisers, printers, shippers, product packaging and other business data can be temporarily obtained for business evaluation and then copied. Since company "N" officially does not participate in the evaluation, the unsuspicious manufacturer may inadvertently (and "free of charge") transfer the valuable information to a competitor.

Even if the data is not physically given for temporary custody, a skillful negotiator (or a team of negotiators) can get a colossal amount of information by discussing or examining the data provided for winning over of temptingly "big" purchase orders.[8] Detailed product or service presentations are a convenient and inexpensive way to absorb the desirable competitor's data.

3. BIDDING WAR

Competing suppliers of a target system or product are invited to submit all pertinent background information in order to choose the "best" one. An open or closed bid system may be used. Obviously, no purchase is necessary. This technique allows the "surveyor" to pick up bits of information from numerous competitors within a short period of time. The "bidding" technique can be successfully repeated.

4. TRADE SHOW EXHIBIT RETENTION

A trade show exhibit is taken apart and pictures of it are taken, overnight. This technique is particularly known to be employed by the former Eastern block and underdeveloped countries hosting Western countries' trade shows and exhibitions.

One of the Sundstrand Corporation executives told a story once of an improperly assembled fuel pump being brought by their company to a seminar for a new product demonstration. The company disregarded the error since the pump was for display only. However, when the company representatives came in the next day to open the display, they noticed that the pump has been assembled correctly. Obviously, someone had taken the pump apart overnight and then put it together the proper way.[9]

5. "DUMMY"/SHELL COMPANIES

A business enterprise does not want anyone to know about the acquisition of a desired product. That enterprise employs a shell company, also called a "dummy", or an underground dealer (middleman) for purchasing a product (or product components) and re-route it to a designated place for final assembly. Thus, the product purchaser remains anonymous. This incognito method was used mostly by companies located in countries against which the trade embargo had been imposed and the final product was used for intrastate (not for export) use.

Illustration:

One American company (Spawr Optical Research, Inc. of Corona, California) shipped laser mirrors needed for the laser weapons to their "final destination", Germany and Switzerland. Then, a European national transported the mirrors to the former Soviet Union.[10]

Illustration:

Another U.S. company (I.I. Industries of Sunnyvale, California) has shipped American computer equipment in crates labeled "washing machines" and "air conditioners" through fictitious companies in Germany, Canada and Switzerland to the former Soviet Union.[11] The Soviets used this intermediary to obtain the forbidden equipment in order to by-pass the U.S. government sale restrictions.

6. COMPUTER HOOK-UP

Dial-up techniques offer a simple route for pillaging or wreaking havoc with valuable databases, or for tapping high-power computers for free use thereof, e.g. to resolve military-related or other problems.

Illustrations of hackers' successful penetration and use of the companies' computer systems:

(1) An ex-employee using his personal computer, and guessing at the passwords of company employees, tapped into the former employer's computer system, obtained the product data and customer list, and used them for marketing the same product at a substantial discount;[12]

(2) a few teenagers broke into a computer system in the nuclear-weapons laboratory using dial-up entry and password search; one of them had only completed a six-week computer course;[13]

(3) a college student gained access to the computer networks of the U.S. Department of Defense and Air Force using his home computer;[14]

(4) the Soviets reached Cray-1 mainframe computer in Britain, from an Austrian research institution, and calculated a nuclear weapons system. Also, in 1981 the Soviet experts tapped into a Lockheed airplane manufacturing database.[15]

7. SCIENTIFIC EXCHANGES

Joint ventures and scientific exchanges with the former Soviet and Third World countries siphon the technical knowledge of the West at the West's expense.

Illustration of the countries' uneven interests in subjects:

Americans studied humanitarian sciences (poetry, dance, etc.) in the communist countries, while former Soviet-block science envoys in the United States gravitated to fields like micro-electronics, computers, float glass, fuel-air explosives, geological studies (pinpointing the location of minerals), medical and cosmetic chemistry, and so forth.[16]

8. VISITING

Seeing, touching, sampling and otherwise absorbing information on tours of a target company provides the purveyor with free intelligence.

Illustrations of a visiting method application:

(1) In one case, foreign engineers touring an aircraft manufacturing facility were wearing shoes with adhesive soles, picking up floor dust and shavings, in order to determine aircraft materials.[17]

(2) In another case, a retiree from the Dow Chemical's Italian subsidiary "accidentally" dropped his handkerchief into a fermentation vat during his farewell visit to the laboratory. Analysis of the bacterial strain, absorbed by the handkerchief, revealed a formula of the antituberculosis drug Rifampicin, which was later sold to a South Korean company.[18]

The "visiting" method is equally applied to restricted and nonrestricted areas of a target company and could be used for absorbing not only physical samples but also for collecting observed data, such as notices on the company's bulletin boards, memoranda and drawings on the employee's desk.

9. INTERCEPTION OF DATA TRANSMISSION

Unscrambled wire, computer-to-computer, facsimile, telephone and satellite transmissions of conversations, computer or other business information may easily be intercepted.

Illustration:

Microwave transmissions (high frequency radio signals) of telephone and facsimile messages are beamed between and beyond reception towers into outer space where they can be intercepted and re-transmitted by satellites. Constantly monitored messages are intercepted when a computer detects a trigger word or phrase and then the entire message is recorded.[19]

The former Eastern bloc agents have reportedly installed automated electronic devices near military installations. The buried robot antennas pop up from the underground only to record the U.S. military messages and transmit them to a passing Soviet satellite.[20]

Furthermore, electromagnetic impulses radiated by the computer cables, computer keystrokes and electronic equipment can be picked by the Van Eck type of devices which duplicate the data onto another computer located away from the data generating equipment. Each computer, printer, facsimile machine and other electronic devices generate electronic impulses which can be intercepted and converted back to the original text or numbers. Computer signals penetrate the walls like radio signals. The technical term used by intelligence communities for this concept is "Tempest." It is difficult to shield the equipment from "Tempest" but for the right price it can be done.[21]

10. INFORMATION BROKERS

Information brokers search through computer databases, contact governmental agencies, private parties, libraries and other information sources in order to find an answer to a posed problem. Some brokers specialize in technical fields, such as chemical or electrical engineering, while others in public relations, marketing or sales. A party may simply pay an information broker for the research of competitors' products, plans or capabilities.

11. PUBLIC AIRWAYS

There is no privacy or secrecy of conversations conducted over cellular phones. An off-the-shelf radio scanner can monitor conversations over cellular phones. Even TV sets made before 1982 can pick up portable or car phone calls because TV stations had used the ultra-high-frequencies (UHF) channels which are now used for portable phone communications. Any conversation over a portable or cellular telephone may be heard by anyone and used by the government agencies to prosecute people for crimes discussed over these telephones. Even eavesdropping laws will not protect the privacy of communications, or respective information, disclosed over or through the public airways.

12. SCIENTIFIC PRESENTATIONS

Press-conferences, scientific reports, speeches to trade groups or interviews may involve discussions of sensitive information. Researchers and engineers trying to stake out their ideas usually disregard and despise any security-related censorship. Consequently, their publications and presentations at symposiums and scientific conferences yield a wealth of information for any interested parties. Friendly discussions with scientists, engineers and conference attendants at a conference is one way to gather technical innovations.

13. EAVESDROPPING

Eavesdropping, either in person or by technical means (audio, optical, video and electronic) is an important tool of industrial spies. Camouflaged cameras, radio transmitters and TV cameras may be installed in phone or electrical outlets (indoor and outdoor), plastic nails embedded in the walls or in the furniture, pagers, cufflinks, shoe heels, jewels or lapel flowers. Eavesdropping equipment is movable, portable and installable in vehicles, ships, airplanes, apartments, hotels, trees or anywhere your imagination can go.

Room and phone "bugging" is one the most pervasive means of data collection. It is very simple to wiretap with "alligator clips" or install wireless microphones which would permit listening to and recording of conversations at a remote place. Besides the above-mentioned tools, there are numerous other listening devices. These gadgets may pick up voice communications off the window glass, walls, etc.

All the necessary equipment for such information interception is commercially available in the U.S.A. and other countries. For instance, more than 2,000 of bugging devices are sold weekly in Britain.[22] Such listening and recording devices are usually installed in the company executives' and technical supervisors' offices, board of directors meeting rooms, and conference rooms.

Eavesdropping is an essential part of the data collection process of private parties and government agencies. Electronic eavesdropping (of calculators, computers, printers and other equipment giving off electronic signals) was noticed by the U.S. Congress, which made steps to make it unlawful.[23]

Illustration:

In 1996, according to the U. S. newspapers, Japan expressed its concerns over a report of CIA eavesdropping on Japanese auto company executives and government officials. The gathered data was used by the U.S. trade representative in Geneva trade negotiations. The U.S. Government refused to comment on these reports but did not deny such activity.[24]

Illustration:

When Russian embassies send to Russia summaries of the intercepted U.S. business telephone communications, the National Security Agency intercepts and deciphers these messages using its sophisticated computers and electronic encrypting devices.[25]

14. OLD-FASHIONED THEFT

Practically anything of business value can be stolen. Theft is taking away the property of another person without the owner's permission. There are many ways to deprive the owner of his property, in this case proprietary information.

Illustrations of reported cases:

(1) A president of a consulting firm was indicted for stealing secret

designs of micro-electronic circuitry (which were shipped to Poland via Austria);[26]

(2) Japanese electronics vendors tried to steal trade secrets from IBM by recruiting IBM employees and former employees;[27]

(3) A Ford Motor Company research engineer was jailed and fined for selling Ford's float-glass technology to a Portuguese company.[28]

These cases demonstrate a continuous search-and-acquire mission by competitors to obtain valuable proprietary data through techniques both sophisticated and crude, such as theft of documents. This "misappropriation" technique can be combined with the "hiring away" method of getting precious business data. Companies are being victimized regardless of their size.

Illustration:

General Motors sued its German competitor, Volkswagen AG, for hundreds of millions of dollars in damages for orchestrating the theft of top secret business plans and product designs. GM alleged that since November 1992, a spy cell including Jose Ignacio Lopez de Arriortua, GM's vice president of worldwide purchasing, and seven of his aides, extracted thousands of confidential documents.

These documents specified new car design components, plans for a secret manufacturing plant called "Plant X", and costs of car parts. About twenty cartons of GM's and Adam Opel AG's (GM's European subsidiary) confidential documents were transported to Volkswagen's headquarters in Wolfburg, Germany, and Lopez's home in Spain via couriers and Volkswagen corporate planes. The documents were then electronically stored and shredded.[29]

The upshot of this alleged activity was that:

(a) VW has used the data to cut the research costs and develop new cars and high-tech facilities;

(b) Lopez's salary jumped from $375,000 at GM to $1.6 million at Volkswagen;

(c) Lopez's aides were hired by VW; and

(d) It has been reported that the suit was settled for one hundred million dollars and VW has agreed to purchase at least $1 billion worth of GM parts within seven years.[30]

15. AERIAL PHOTOGRAPHY

Satellites with high-resolution cameras and private airplanes equipped with built-in cameras can take aerial photographs of a targeted plant.

Illustration:

Private photographers were hired to conduct aerial photography of a DuPont plant which was under construction and, thus, exposed to view from the above construction area. Photographs of the plant and equipment, which were designed to produce methanol by a highly secret but unpatented process, would enable a skilled person to deduce that secret process.[31]

Illustration:

The state-of-the-art cameras take pictures from miles away with amazing clarity and sharpness. The satellite cameras can pick up details as small as a license plate number or faces of people. Target objects can be seen (through the windows) inside the building, or, if brought outside the building, through the product's transparent covers. For years, the Soviet intelligence satellites were taking pictures of secret facilities, such as the buildings which housed the Skunk Works teams. Russians knew that these teams were developing the next generation space shuttle, the X-33 VentureStar for the Lockheed Martin Corporation. Satellite cameras allowed Russians to continuously and nonintrusively monitor the target facilities. Among other things, satellite photos of cars on the facilities' parking lots allowed the Soviets to count the number of people working on that project.[32]

16. INFILTRATION

A target company can be infiltrated by an agent posing either as a temporary or full time employee. A "mole" with good professional credentials can apply for an advertised job opening and work for the target company for a long time. A mole, who could be a scientist, secretary, or senior administrator, may either continuously feed information or commit one monumental act or transaction which would undermine the target company's competitive posture or values.

17. JOB INTERVIEWS

A scientist, designer or a key employee of a target company is approached (via a telephone call or letter) by an independent employment agency. A representative of the agency, familiar with that employee's personal and professional background, offers a unique job opportunity with a big company. The position, money, and benefits are great. The company may or may not be named. If the company identity is not disclosed, the explanation is that this is done in order to avoid a direct contact with the employing company. Otherwise, the commission of the employment agency may be lost.

The employee meets with that representative in a restaurant or a hotel business suite. During the interview the employee is asked about his or her technical background, current projects and inner structure of the target company. Fake interviews with one or more employees result in the collection of data on the business and marketing plans of the target company.[33]

18. USED EQUIPMENT MARKET

The U.S. equipment sold to its allies under a valid export license can be repurchased by anyone as a used equipment. Such repurchase may take place within a few months after the initial purchase of the equipment by either a "friendly" business enterprise or a shell company. This technique is employed by the companies which, due to a trade embargo or export restrictions, cannot buy the products directly from the U.S. manufacturers. Most of the equipment can be legally purchased on the open market. U.S. agencies cannot control such sales due to the sheer volume of such transactions. Another reason is that other nations would fill in the gap if the sale is blocked.

Illustrations:

(1) The Kama River truck complex manufactures military trucks using legally acquired American technology.[34]

(2) Sermetel, Inc., a Pennsylvania firm, legally sold the technology for applying ceramic coatings to jet engines. However, when U.S. officials discovered that such technology would greatly reduce engine overhaul time and, thus, increase the effectiveness of the Warsaw Pact air forces, the sale was stopped.[35]

19. MISAPPLICATION OF FIELD OF USE

A product or system designed to do something in one (civilian) field of use can be utilized in another (military) field. This misapplication method is applied by companies to get around the restrictions imposed on the sale of sophisticated equipment.

Illustration:

The Bryant Chucking Grinder Co., a Vermont company, sold 164 precision grinding machines to the former Soviet Union (in 1972). The machines enabled the Soviets to produce ball bearings which significantly improved the accuracy of the missile guidance system for their intercontinental missiles. As a result of improved missile accuracy, the United States had to spend billions of dollars in order to fortify the land-based missile sites and design MX "shell game" for stationing the MX missiles.[36]

Illustration:

In early 1985, Consarc Engineering, LTD., a Scottish subsidiary of Consarc Corp., in Rancocas, New Jersey, sold equipment for making a carbon-carbon material to the former Soviet Union. The material significantly improved the accuracy of Russian nuclear warheads by reducing the warheads' wobble and drag while passing through the atmosphere. Western governments could have stopped the sale of the equipment but did not.[37]

20. BLACKMAIL

Drugs, women, money and various legal or illegal favors are the most traditional ways to trap the "target". Loss of prestige, family problems, career dissatisfaction or financial dire straits prompt some people to betray their employer and their country.

Illustration:

A 14-year employee of National Security Agency (Ronald Pelton) sold to the Soviets certain U.S. military secrets (how the NSA intercepts, decodes and analyzes secret Soviet communications), valued at millions of dollars, for $35,000. He stated in court that his financial predicament prompted such a betrayal.[38]

Blackmail is usually initiated with the "target" through love affairs, "easy" loans, emigration visas and marriage certificates for the proposed spouses in other countries, road accidents and phoney charges of crimes committed by foreigners traveling within the communist countries. These techniques were successfully used by the former East Germany. According to the West German government, East Germany had at least 3,000 people in West Germany who were working as agents and passing documents to East Germans from their place of work.[39]

21. WOMEN: INTELLIGENCE AGENTS

An agent collecting information stealthily is usually depicted by the media as a charismatic man. However, female agents can be very effective in obtaining information in a male-dominated social, military, industrial and political circles. Female agents are trained to be "swallows" whose function is to trick a target into a love affair. The love affair is recorded with hidden cameras, and the pictures or videotapes are used for blackmail. Out-of-town businessmen who came to trade shows or conferences (their names are registered and circulated among other attendants) want to have a good time. Businessmen, entangled in the entertainment and socializing environment surrounding these business meetings, are targeted for blackmail purposes.

Women trained by intelligence services are especially devastating, in all senses of the word, in their assignments. They may pose as journalists, students, secretaries, stewardesses, consulate workers, trade organization or airline representatives. Agents are trained to extort information, seduce, survive any weather condition without food or shelter, and kill using any available means, including over-the-counter poisons, acids, incendiary devices, ropes, forks, nails and martial arts' techniques. They are well versed in the literature, arts and social structure of a target country. These beautiful and intelligent women can easily start relationships leading to a sex-for-secrets trap, blackmail and the murder, if necessary, of a target party. The agents' notions of remorse, pity and compassion are replaced with the paramount devotion to the motherland and instinctive subordination to their superiors and their orders.

However, women themselves can be recruited by using the same orthodox sex-for-secret method.

Illustration:

A secretary who had worked for twenty-six years for West German presidents, conveyed to the KGB information on the secret storage of chemical weapons in West Germany, missile deployment in Europe, and Western evaluation of Soviet government conflicts. She took pictures (by a camera in a lipstick case) of at least 1,717 classified documents, and informed the Soviets about West Germany's foreign intelligence activities. She did this all in the name of love for an East German boyfriend who gave her presents, paid her about $16,500, and vacationed with her in Europe.[40]

Endless number of men were "charmed" by swallows, including diplomats, executives, scientists and American servicemen.

22. TOY MODELS

Information may be leaked through cracks, even in the most sophisticated security system set up by defense contractors. The leaks may take the most unsual and unexpected form, such as a toy model.

Illustrations:

(1) A toy model of the supersecret Stealth fighter airplane of Lockheed Corp. became an instant commercial success because it represented an accurate copy of the actual airplane. The toy manufacturer gathered the plane details from trade magazines, a sketch submitted to him by a commercial pilot who had observed the airplane at the air force's test site, and personal contacts with engineers in the aerospace industry.[41]

(2) Once, Admiral Rickover decried that a $2.98 children's toy of a nuclear submarine was made authentic in every detail to an actual submarine inner structure. This was definitely a multi-million dollar freebie to anyone who is interested in building nuclear submarines.[42]

23. EMPLOYEES

Disgruntled employees seeking another job may disclose to prospective employers valuable information or they may sell this information in return for money, sex or drugs. Former employees who set up their own shops in competition with the employer, or who began working for a competitor, may knowingly or inadvertently disclose or use the former employer's proprietary information.

24. CUSTOMERS

Even loyal customers can relay confidential data or proprietary information to competitors.

Illustration of a commercial secret disclosure by a loyal customer:

Forthcoming price discounts, a new slogan or trademark may be learned by a customer and easily picked up by the competition through direct or indirect contact (for example, through a relative or a common friend) with this customer. Such disclosure may lead to a pre-emptive strike by a competitor. If a competitor knows that, on a certain date, the McDonald's Corporation intends to introduce a new product or lower the price of an existing product, the competitor may offer a lower price or an identical product prior to that introduction date.

25. REAL ESTATE AGENCIES

Commercial and industrial real estate listings and leases may disclose certain costs and plant layouts. Real estate brokers usually convey to prospective purchasers or lessees the requested data about the target company with a hope of the impending deal consummation. Brokers may also secure the company's data upon the prospect's request.

A potential purchaser of a business property may glean business data during negotiations to buy, sell, or rent that business property. In compliance with the potential "buyer" or "lessee" request, a real estate agent may obtain information as to equipment layouts, expenses, liens, and so forth.

26. UNSOLICITED IDEA SUBMISSIONS

The company may be forced to litigate and disclose sensitive information if they commercially use a non-employee's unsolicited idea. The idea must be novel, disclosed in confidence, and sufficiently concrete.[43]

Illustration of the unsolicited idea submission technique:

An "outsider" sends an invention or innovative business idea to the target company. The company may have similar ideas or projects under development for years prior to that submission. Nevertheless, if the company improperly rejects the submitted innovation, does not document the evaluation of the submission, or accepts it without a waiver of confidentiality, then all related business data may be exposed and collected via a litigation process. The "outsider" may file an unfair competition, trade secret misappropriation, breach of contract or other lawsuits trying to recover money and forcing the company to disclose its research, marketing and accounting data.

27. ADVERTISING AND SALES LITERATURE

Marketing personnel's earnest efforts to sell the company's products and/or services through advertising, sales and promotional literature may unnecessarily disclose secret material or technical facts.

Illustration of possible loss of technical data via promotional literature:

An unpatented process disclosure, or novel product application, may be misappropriated by a competitor who may improve upon or slightly modify the structure embodying that innovation and then patent it. This may even preclude the original party from product sale expansion or totally shut down the respective product manufacturing.

28. U.S. GOVERNMENT

Government officials leak information to the media on purpose and also disclose the information unintentionally.

Illustration of unintentional, perhaps negligent, information dissemination:

According to *U.S. News & World Report,* the State Department's Office of Foreign Buildings gave drawings for the renovation of the U.S. Embassy, bombed in East Beirut, to a printing company. That company then sold them to at least eleven Lebanese construction firms (at $250.00 apiece) that did not have security clearances.[44]

Illustration of intentional disclosure of sensitive information:

According to a survey of top government officials from the Johnson administration to the Reagan administration, 42% of them intentionally leaked information to the press in order to advance a particular issue, to rebut false information, or to gain support from nongovernmental groups.[45]

The cheapest way to obtain secret business information is simply to request that the U.S. government supply it under the Freedom of Information Act (FOIA). Under the Freedom of Information Act, any person may obtain information which is not statutorily exempted from disclosure. The party who is obliged to supply sensitive information to the government is not in control of information being disclosed to the information requesters.

In 1983, the Pentagon responded fully to more than 60,000 (out of 72,000) requests and the Justice Department answered completely to more than half of 24,000 applications. Requesters demanded the release of the names of government informants as well as U.S. agents in the former Eastern block countries; individual's CIA and FBI files; declassification of documents (because the government can be persuaded); business secrets; and so forth.[46]

Any person (including foreigners) can request any record held by a government agency. Although trade secrets and financial information obtained by a government agency fall within the nine disclosure exemptions under the FOIA, the government agencies still must respond to all requests. The requesters are under no obligation to state why the information is being requested.

Upon receipt of the request, the government agency must notify the business about such request in order to give them opportunity to comment or claim confidentiality for proprietary information. If the company's reply is not received promptly or trade secrets are not identified properly, the data leakage may occur.

The FOIA may aid in obtaining proprietary information by competitors which take advantage of such a data collection avenue.

Illustration:

British automakers, Swedish ball-bearing manufacturers, French aviation companies and many other companies used FOIA to get valuable information. A pharmaceutical concern, Pfizer, alleged that in 1982 more than four-fifth of the 34,000 FOIA requests for information received by the Food and Drug Administration were business secret inquiries.[47]

There are endless government publications that are available both in paper and in electronic form (through the databases and CD-ROM disks). One may access, print and save official government documents (full text and graphics) exactly as they appear in print format through the Internet. For example, free government information can be obtained from the Federal Register, Congressional Bills, GAO Reports, Public Laws and other publications appearing on-line at the World Wide Web site of the U.S. Government Printing Office, WAIS Server (http://www.access.gpo.gov/su_docs/aces/aaces002.html).

Federal and state publications dispense a colossal amount of free information on hundreds of subjects. One may get Food and Drug Administration Records, reports of Office of Technology Assessment, Federal Communication Commission's Telephone and Radio Equipment lists. The *Monthly Catalog of U.S. Government Publications* and *The Index to Government Periodicals* identify all federal publications. *The U.S. Government Manual* summarizes each agency's role, lists the executives names with their addresses and phone numbers. The "Federal Register" is the medium for federal regulations, notices, public laws and rules. The list is very extensive. Also, government employees may find out and provide an inquirer with free information on competitors' products, services, locations, contacts, etc. For example, one may get assistance for all GPO (the Government Printing Office) electronic products from the User Support Team by calling a toll-free number 1-888-293-6498; or through the Internet e-mail: gpoaccess@gpo.gov.

In short, the U.S. government is one of the most prolific suppliers of business data which can be acquired by anyone at a minimal cost or no cost at all.

29. SUPPLIERS

Suppliers use the confidential information of a customer to do analogous work, or supply the same parts and material for another customer. This translates into giving technical and price data to a customer's competitor. This also enables the competitor to acquire the supplier-developed technology quicker and at a lower price thereby benefiting from the investment made by the original customer.

30. RECORD RETENTION

Failure to keep track of records and data given to other parties for evaluation represents a breach of security. Such failure may be capitalized on by data recipients. Sensitive information given to prospective purchasers or licensees (even with appropriate precautions) is not retrieved, or even requested to be returned to the owner, upon a breakdown in the negotiations.

31. PREMATURE TESTING OR DISPLAY

Experimental field testing of a new product, or market testing by displaying the actual model of a product to potential customers, reveals not only the product features and tips off the competition, but it also may preclude the product owner from obtaining patent protection for the product.

Field-tested products may not be sufficiently camouflaged or dis-
guised when brought outside the manufacturing facilities. Uncovered
products also communicate to the public the product features for
either the publicity, quality control or market research related to that
product.

32. LAWSUITS AND COURT RECORDS

Court records may disclose certain data which companies are obliged
to provide and which they cannot control thereafter. Although the
sensitive information may be withdrawn from public disclosure by
protective orders, review of the court records may yield a wealth of
technical, marketing and personnel information about the corporate
litigants. This is an inexpensive way to get information from a competitor.

Illustration of the litigation sieve:

In response to interrogatories (opposing party's questions which must
be answered under oath), notice to produce documents and things,
and oral discovery (depositions, i.e. interrogations by attorneys) in a
lawsuit, companies may name their suppliers, customers, prices, marketing plans, designers and many other things which otherwise would
not be disclosed. Suits involving unfair competition, patent or trademark infringement, bankruptcy and reorganization are the most
revealing sources of company business, technical and marketing data.

33. TRADE SHOWS

Sales people socialize with each other at trade shows and exchange
their knowledge of their own or other competitors' products, and
business or marketing plans. Trade shows present the best opportuni-

ties for the recruitment of agents and the informal gathering of corporate intelligence and innovations.

Trade shows bring together the latest designs of all products in a particular field and, therefore, give a company plenty of opportunities to learn what the competition is doing. Sales people are happy to discuss technical details with curious "customers" who may ask about the product specifications and characteristics, prices and availability of such or other products on the market. Premature display of a product, in order to solicit sales before actual production of a product, gives the competition an advance look at the product.

34. TECHNICAL PUBLICATIONS

Continuous review of publications in the industry magazines, newsletters and association circulars disclose valuable marketing and technical information. Sales and promotional literature, announcements, owner manuals, extensive product specifications, professional meetings and research reports constitute valuable sources of information. Intracompany newsletters and publications distributed to employees can be analyzed along with the engineering or technical presentations made by company employees at scientific conferences or published in trade journals, business and engineering school papers.

As a rule, engineers and scientists are more concerned with their name recognition and commercial success than with the security or protection of their ideas and inventions. Hence, the time, money and human resources, needed to digest and implement the freely available information are the only limitations on parties gathering data.

Every business school requires students to prepare case studies based on real facts and situations. Such case study and the faculty staff's articles are published in the school journals.

Illustration:

A student at the Massachusetts Institute of Technology, Cambridge, Massachusetts, submitted a paper on a new ship-propulsion system based on the penguin flipper's flapping motion and fish wiggling movements compensating the weakness of fish muscles. The four-motor system comprises flippers producing flapping and twisting motions. This discovery may become a technical solution to Gray's Paradox (biologist James Gray's observation that the power of fish muscles is three to seven times lower than the power needed to swim) and revolutionize ship construction.

A test model has reached eighty seven percent efficiency in comparison to forty to seventy percent efficiency of conventional propeller-driven watercraft. Mass production of such flipper-driven watercraft would save the Navy and commercial shipping industry millions of gallons of fuel and respective amounts of money.[48]

Careful review of the technical publications may reveal fresh ideas and analyses of the trade or industry products.

35. EXCESSIVE DISSEMINATION

Dissemination of information to rank-and-file employees who do not participate in a decision-making process, or do not need to know such information, inescapably leads to a leak of information.

Illustration of excessive information distribution:

Memoranda or announcements disclosing the product technical specifications or names of the acquisition targets distributed to assembly line workers may end up in the hands of representatives of competitors. This will result in giving away the product introduction lead time or other benefits.

36. POLLS AND MARKET SURVEYS

Surveys, polls, and market researches conducted by agencies (hired by competitors or even by noncompetitors) may include secret data gathering questions. Detailed questionnaires (containing the significant interrogatories buried in the body of the questionnaire) may uncover the size, ability, and intentions of the target company.

Market surveys, and various polls which extract opinion and information from suppliers, customers, business executives and managers may reveal a wealth of information about the competition. There are research agencies specializing in gathering of such corporate intelligence. Market researchers are particularly good for specific assignments, such as learning about the competitor's new product introduction date.

Customers may respond to questions posed in printed questionnaires or in friendly discussions with the sales people as to the competitor's products. Sales "calls" or field reports can be analyzed in order to determine customers' reaction to new ideas and products.

37. CASUAL CONVERSATIONS

Casual talks with family members, neighbors, friends, and strangers may trigger a chain of communication contacts which one may not foresee or block. A friend has a friend who has a friend, and so on. Even an oral condition of confidentiality extracted from a friend, or a family member, is not a guarantee of nondisclosure of data to their respective spouses, parents, or acquiantances. Also, casual conversations can be overheard by strangers or surveillance teams.

38. CONSULTANTS

Business, management and engineering consultants, including former security officers and government officials, will sell information about: competitor's products, comparison of product compositions; political and socioeconomical conditions in other countries; management; energy saving and marketing techniques; and so forth. Consultants advising the competitors can be "re-used" (employed) to get the benefits of their work for other companies.

Consultants may inadvertently disclose to the competition results of a project they had worked on for another company. They may also sell information which was developed as a result of their contacts or work products. In addition, they can be engaged for corporate intelligence collection, thereby utilizing their specific knowledge, sources and experience.

Illustration of corporate data pilferage or destruction:

A computer consultant working on a computer network and fixing the data management system may be "negligent" in keeping the business data given to him in confidence. The computer consultant can also glean computer-stored data which was not given to him. Such data may find its way to competitors of that business. The consultant may plant a logic bomb or a virus into a computer system which may be triggered by a predetermined event in the future.

39. PROSPECTIVE LICENSEES

Prospective licensees or buyers may use, modify or disseminate information about the facilities, capabilities, product development and manufacturing methods, that may not be covered by nondisclosure agreements. Prospective licensees have the right to inquire about minute details of the licensed technology. Disclosure can turn into a disaster for the target company if the disclosed informaton is not properly documented and restricted.

40. PACKAGING

Packaging may disclose names of suppliers, product ingredients, plant locations, plant capacity (which may be figured out by counting the number of shipments), and other data. Packaging is difficult to protect from observation by unintended parties but proper coding can impair the supplier and product data collection.

41. REVERSE ENGINEERING

It is perfectly legal to take apart a commercially available product in order to reconstruct a similar product, a process called reverse engineering. Trade secrets can be learned through reverse engineering from publicly available products. For example, taking apart and analyzing a competitor's car, which was bought on the open market, is a routine procedure followed by motor vehicle manufacturers.

The reverse engineering method of data collection is applied not only to mechanical contraptions but also to discovery of food, material and fluid ingredients, and other chemical and physical characteristics of a product.

Illustration of a chemical reverse engineering method application:

Designer scents, such as Calvin Klein's Obsession ($28 for 1.7 ounces), can be chemically reverse engineered, simulated and sold by competitors.[49] Parfumes de Klein Cosmetics spent $17.5 million to introduce and promote the product "Obsession". The company tried to stop the copycats by filing numerous unfair competition lawsuits.

But successful interception of copycat competition becomes very difficult if a competitor uses technical means to decipher the product ingredients, such as a gas chromatograph for breaking down the original perfume formula. This chemical deciphering or reverse engineering is legal, or, in other words, no misappropriation of the secret formula has occurred. However, legally reverse-engineered products still may infringe patents, copyrights, and may violate trademark protection laws.

Practically all corporate information is publicly available for legal skimming through reverse engineering. Most companies do this routinely. It is the acquisition and copying of the product without the consent of the owner that makes such activity unlawful.

Illustration of illegal reverse engineering:

A Soviet sonar buoy, discovered in waters off North Carolina, had a circuit board which was identical to a U.S.-manufactured device carried in submarine tracking sonar buoys of the U.S. Navy.[50] Since such sonar buoys were not commercially available to Russians, it can be assumed that the means used to obtain the buoy design were improper.

Sometimes, trade secret protection may be denied by a court.

Illustration of trade secret loss:

Manufacturing information pertaining to a "Commando" armored personnel carrier was held not to be a trade secret because the alleged secrets were reverse engineered, or they were available in trade literature.[51]

42. LICENSING

All intangible assets, such as patents, trademarks, copyrights, trade secrets, know-how or technical assistance can be licensed separately or in combination. Licenses can be exclusive (even preventing the licensor to practice the invention, unless agreed otherwise) or nonexclusive (giving a licensee the right to use the invention without being sued for infringement).

A license may restrict the use, manufacture, or sale of the underlying property, and the territory may be split between different licensees. But the bottom line is that the licensor shares its technological achievements with the licensees in return for royalties. Therefore, in order to get the most advanced or desirable product, or service, one may buy it in small increments, as royalties, or in a lump sum.

For example, South Korea applied its licensed technology so successfully that it now can produce high-quality personal computers and compete in the most advanced computer-related areas.

43. FRANCHISING

A franchise is just another kind of a trademark, service mark, or trade name license which gives the franchisor the vast authority to control the franchisee's operation, marketing and other business-related matters.[52]

A license is a permission to make, sell or use a product without imposing any limitations, except maybe quality control, over the business operation of the licensee. A franchise is the same license plus restrictions designed to ensure the uniformity and standard of service. Retailers or dealers have the same relationship with distributors as franchisors with franchisees.

Most states have statutes that require the filing of copies of all disclosure agreements, advertisements and franchise agreements with the Secretary of State or similar governmental agency. That information is public and accessible to anyone. Franchising is a means to gather new data and learn advanced service and business techniques.

44. JOINT VENTURES

One of the more economical ways to participate in the technology evolution is to join the competition in a joint research and development venture. The joint venture aggregates the resources, accelerates the product development, permits more efficient use of all facilities and equipment, combines the skills and know-how of all participants, and spreads the risk if the project is not successful. If the project is successful, the participating companies cross-license each other as to the developed information and incorporate the obtained results in their respective products.

45. EMPLOYMENT ADVERTISEMENT

Job advertisements can reveal what skills the company needs to pursue certain business projects. For example, if a tractor manufacturing company seeks aerospace vehicle designers, that kind of employee search may give away the company's future plans.

Employment agency may provide information about the company and their plans. Monitoring the display advertisements will yield facts about projected products, plant locations, specialties needed, changes in marketing plans, and plant hiring patterns.

46. PATENTS

Patents disclose the concept and the best mode of operation of an invention which was available to inventors at the time of filing a patent application. Careful study of the competitor's patents and all prior art references cited during the prosecution of the patent, which are gathered in the patent file history ("file wrapper"), reveal new ideas and direction in which the competitor is heading. The above-mentioned information is available to any member of the public.

After learning what the patent contemplates, one may adopt the concept, but modify the structure or process covered by the patent claims, so as not to infringe the patent. Patent attorneys help their clients to determine whether their product infringes a patent and how to design around the claimed invention.

Sometimes it is impractical or difficult to design around the patented product or method. Another route to end the patent protection is to invalidate the patent by asserting that:

(a) the invention was anticipated or obvious in view of the newly found prior art; or

(b) fraud was committed on the Patent Office; or

(c) the application was filed more than a year after it was offered for sale or publicly used; or

(d) other patent invalidation arguments which patent attorneys are the most familiar with.

A relatively inexpensive procedure, called a "re-examination," may be invoked in order to invalidate the patent. An anonymous party may initiate such a procedure in the U.S. Patent and Trademark Office by submitting additional prior art references and requesting the re-examination of a particular patent.

If the patent is found to be invalid, then anyone is free to use the patented invention. Properly collected data is used to eliminate a competitor's defense of their innovation, as well as to improve upon or modify (design around) the patented invention.

47. YELLOW PAGES

Yellow Pages advertisements yield limited but useful information. Using these advertisements, one may compile a list of company locations, learn the names and number of competitors, trace suppliers and distributors, and so forth. Each bit of information is compiled as a jigsaw puzzle for a complete analytical review of the corporate business data.

48. SHAREHOLDERS' MEETINGS

One may attend the stockholders' meetings of a public company and learn facts brought up by shareholders. The executives also discuss company strategies, product specifications, supplier and marketing data. Many questions asked at the meeting, including disputes with the company's executives, may bring to life the secret intentions of the management team.

49. PLANT OBSERVATION

Plant observation allows one to learn the name of the product component suppliers and packaging manufacturers to determine supply shipments and, consequently, sales figures. This technique may be used to count employees entering the facilities in order to determine the reduction of or increase in the company's labor force. One may also take pictures of the components or assembled products being loaded onto trucks, packaged, or otherwise exposed to uninhibited observation thereof.

50. TRADE PUBLICATIONS

Various magazines, directories, indexes, statistical sources may disclose valuable data. Each topic may be covered in hundreds of directories and data sources. The following is a short list of directories containing the corporate background information:

(a) Internet. Science and industry sources, business advertising, target company data, and declassified military data may be found on the Internet. See Section 74 ("Internet") below.

(b) Value Line, Standard and Poor's, or Dun & Bradstreet reports detail corporate financial and owner profiles, product, management and employee population data.

(c) Lawyer's Desk Reference reveals the identity of experts who could be employed as consultants for data gathering or analysis in numerous fields, public organizations, etc.

51. LABOR UNION PUBLICATIONS

Newsletters and announcements circulated among union members contain business plans of various companies regarding closing plants, mergers, company profits or losses, layoffs, employment, plant relocation, bankruptcy, lawsuits against the company and so forth.

52. LOCAL NEWSPAPERS

Reporters trying to break the news or conduct an analysis of the industry, product, or company do extensive research which can be used for corporate intelligence. Meticulous study of local as well national newspapers on a continuous basis, or by assignment, is a legitimate data collection means. This technique can be extensively used for gleaning nontechnical information.

53. FOREIGN COUNTERPARTS OF U.S. PUBLICATIONS

The study of foreign publications in respective trade, science and industry areas combined with other data may create a different picture of the competitor strength and weaknesses than portrayed by the U.S. media. Sometimes it is cheaper to get needed information by employing foreign intellectuals (consultant sources) and conducting foreign publication research abroad than to employ analogous consultants in the United States.

54. THE U.S. PATENT AND TRADEMARK OFFICE (U.S.P.T.O.)

This source may be employed to learn about latest inventions, patentees, patent numbers, abstracts of the inventions, assignee's name, U.S. class and subclass classification, trademark and class of goods or services, owner and registration number of a trademark. The U.S.P.T.O. on-line databases and associated patent-related publications ("Official Gazette", "U.S. Patents Quarterly", etc.) are very useful for litigators, engineers and researchers.

55. INDEX OF PATENT ASSIGNEES

This index identifies the current owners of patents who bought, or otherwise obtained, ownership rights to patented inventions.

56. CUSTOMS BROKERS

The majority of products coming into the United States pass through the customs brokers, who help arrange temporary container (delivered goods) storage, payment of duties, etc. They know the tariffs in their country for imported merchandise. Brokers are familiar with the product features and new product introduction schedules. Their knowledge may be used for getting information on importers.

57. DISTRIBUTORS AND RETAILERS

The retailers and distributors have information from different sources and personal contacts. Their knowledge may help the inquirer learn about the competitors' pricing, discount policies, new displays, product delivery schedules, advertising, dates of expected new product shipments, and so forth.

58. STOCK ANALYSTS

Practically every brokerage house has a research department which conducts studies regarding business activities of numerous companies. Stock brokers have access to that research and may get reams of companies' financial and business data based on interviews with the target company management, market surveys, new product lines and product introduction dates.

59. CREDIT REPORTS

Credit reports show sales, debts and revenue data provided by creditors and the target company itself. Judgments entered against the company, lawsuits, nonpayment or late payment of bills for services rendered, or goods purchased, and loan defaults are reflected in the company's or individual's credit record.

60. ANNUAL REPORTS

Corporate annual reports contain financial statements, identify current lawsuits, delineate business outlook and past performance. Annual reports must disclose to stockholders or prospective stock purchasers, the names of corporate officers and directors, market and dividend information, consolidated balance sheets and statements of income, changes in financial condition, earnings, operating data, and a report by an independent certified public accounting firm.

61. U.S. SECURITY AND EXCHANGE COMMISSION (SEC)

Publicly held corporations must file (under the Securities Exchange Act, 15 U.S.C. 77, et seq., of 1934) a current registration statement with the SEC for securities being offered to the public. A registration statement provides description of major contracts and reveals audited financial statements and agreements underlying the securities offered.

Corporations are also required to file 10-K reports which disclose a list and description of all subsidiaries, the sources of raw materials, locations of company facilities, identity of directors, net revenues and profits.

Publicly held corporations must also file 10-Q quarterly statements, an initial prospectus (describing company's owners, management team, etc.) and proxy statements. Seemingly innocuous numbers provided in the company reports tell a lot to those who know how to use them.

Illustration of a financial statement review application:

Let us analyze one data element, namely, "profit," and see what knowledge of the company's profits may yield. If a parts supplier has high profits on a particular item, a company may:

(a) become a manufacturer of that part, or in other words, become a competitor of the supplier; or

(b) seek another supplier; or

(c) negotiate a lower price from that supplier.

Low profits indicate a financial weakness in certain areas, which competition may utilize by lowering the product prices and driving the company out of business. High profits may show a supplier that the target company may afford higher prices for the supplied product or service. Excessively high profits may indicate an illegal monopoly or unfair competition methods. This may result in antitrust lawsuits by competitors. Cost data may also expose the cheap source of supplies.

62. STATE RECORDS

States maintain public archives, such as Secretary of State depositories, which contain documents filed by companies both voluntarily and in compliance with state laws. These records disclose unpublicized facts.

Illustration of unpublicized facts:

For a small fee one may find out about the company's debts and mechanic's liens claimed by contractors. The Uniform Commercial Code (UCC) filings reveal commercial loan information. Private corporation filings include occupational safety reports, securities, annual reports, trade name registration, franchise tax return, articles of merger and consolidation, and environmental impact statements.

63. SURVEILLANCE OF EXECUTIVES

Surveillance of key employees of a competing company may disclose marketing and business plans, merger, acqusition or divestiture discussions, bargaining position during the negotiation of a business transaction, product introduction date and technological innovations. Surveillance team members monitor cellular phone communications, business trip arrangements, eavesdrop on conversations in public places and hotel rooms, record meetings with representatives of other companies, of selected officials or managers.

Illustration of one of the surveillance techniques:

A chief executive officer (CEO) of a large concern uses every second of his time for work on business-related matters. The CEO makes arrangements through a travel agency to fly to a meeting with an advertising agency. In flight, the CEO is constantly talking on his portable telephone and airphone, typing memos on his laptop computer and reviewing documents for the meeting with the advertising executives.

The CEO engulfed into his work did not realize that his flight and seat numbers were picked up by the surveillance team either through a travel agency or airline (under false pretexts), or eavesdropping on his cellular telephone, or other means. The CEO also did not notice that a nice old lady sitting on the plane right behind him has video recorded his laptop computer screen while he was using the computer, telephone numbers he dialed, documents he studied, "airfone" and cellular telephone conversations with his office and his lover. Such videotape provides the surveillance team employer with product pricing, financial problems, marketing plans, blackmail possibilities and commercial secret records which could not be purchased or accessed to otherwise.

64. FINANCIAL AND INVESTMENT REPORTS

Financial and investment newsletters, journals, and reports published by small private companies and big institutional advisers provide detailed company information. These reports are continuously updated with newest changes. Anyone can purchase reports about the target company via the Dun & Bradstreet and Standard & Poor's reports, brokerage houses or individual investment newsletters and publications.

Illustration of financial report benefits:

Usefulness of such reports may be illustrated by a history of one lawsuit. During litigation, it became apparent that, in order to meet legal requirements and keep the parent company as a defendant in that suit, the tight connection between the accused subsidiary and its parent corporation had to be proven. The Dun & Bradstreet financial reports for these companies revealed that:

(a) both companies shared the same directors and officers;

(b) 100% of the capital stock of the subsidiary was owned by its parent;

(c) advertising and sales of the subsidiary's products were made through the parent company's distributors, representatives, and direct sales force;

(d) a few years ago the parent company explicitly stated in its corporate resolution that the business of the subsidiary corporation is substantially an incident of the business of the parent company; and

(e) the parent company assumed liability for the discharge of absolutely all contractual obligations of the subsidiary.

All of the above mentioned factors reinforced the other party's legal position that both companies were tightly intertwined so as to form one economic unit. Therefore, the parent company became a liable party in the suit. The upshot of this story is that a careful analysis of one financial background report may financially collapse or cause severe damage to a competitor.

65. INTERVIEWS WITH REPORTERS

Radio, TV and newspaper reporter interviews with company officials may reveal publicly unavailable information. Also, company representative's interviews with authors of "pending" books and stock market analysts may yield sensitive data to curious observers.

66. COMMERCIAL DATABASES

Innumerable databases can be used to search for topical articles, patents and specific information about goods or services. There are about five thousand commercial databases worldwide and that number is growing. Almost anyone can access the databases without rigorous inquiries as to the dialer's identity. CD-ROM based data is sold to subscribers by the database owners. An on-line search of American and foreign databases is available to any researcher. Internet searches have become a routine practice for any researcher, since the amount of information available is astonishing.

Illustration of commercial databases:

ACCESS - European Patent Office database of patents and patentees;
LEXIS-NEXIS - case law, reports, statutes, articles;
WESTLAW - court decisions, federal and state statutes;
U.S. PATENT AND TRADEMARK OFFICE - patents, trademarks, patentees, patent assignees.

67. BANKS

Banks, domestic and particularly foreign, provide customers with investment advice and business or marketing data for a respective product or a target company. In order to obtain personal information on potential extortion targets or get the first-hand knowledge of the companies' merger, divestiture or financial plans, a private party may buy a bank to collect such data. Loan applicants must disclose to the bank their financial history, loan purposes and repayment plans in connection with new ventures or payment of old debts. This information is valuable corporate intelligence.

Illustration of a bank acquisition method for information manipulation and economic leverage:

The Soviets used this technique a few years ago. Moscow Narodny Bank gave 70 million dollars in letters of credit, through a Hong Kong middleman, for the purchase of the Peninsula National Bank of Burlingame located near the Silicon Valley in California. Many computer scientists and designers working in the Silicon Valley, the Mecca of the U.S. computer industry, used that bank. Knowledge of their financial situation could make them potential blackmail targets. The deal collapsed when the role and name of the buying principal came to light.[53]

68. U.S. CHAMBERS OF COMMERCE

The United States Chamber of Commerce maintains offices in most countries around the world. These offices are extremely helpful to American businessmen trying to get data about a foreign or domestic company, goods or services. Besides databases containing local business data, the offices provide a lot of useful information that is difficult to obtain outside the foreign country, such as local contacts, customs, needs, bureaucratic procedures, and so forth.

69. FOREIGN CHAMBERS OF COMMERCE AND TRADE ORGANIZATIONS

The foreign counterparts of the U.S. Chamber of Commerce are also extremely helpful to business inquirers. Their personnel will respond to telephone and facsimile inquiries about foreign company's capacity, product line, number of employees, and subsidiaries. At the very least, they will send a photocopy of the local Yellow Pages containing the requested service providers or product suppliers.

70. TRASH EVALUATION

Search and collection of trash may reveal corporate plans, cash flow information, plant capacity, average hourly production rate, collective bargaining agreements, material and labor costs, etc. It is legal in some states to gather information from discarded refuse. However, using the competitor's drawings and parts dumped into garbage and building a product from them may also be considered a theft, i.e. misappropriation of trade secrets, in some states.[54]

Illustration of successful garbage perusal:

A financial analyst of a manufacturer of caskets and hospital beds used the trash collection technique for gathering intelligence on competitors' production schedule and volume, supplier's prices, material and labor costs, corporate plans and research secrets. Using his accounting background and FBI training, he analyzed public information, such as corporate reports filed with the Securities and Exchange Commission. He searched the garbage material for tidbits of information on acquisition and merger plans, plant production rate and capacity, shipping routes, supplier identity, supplier charges, business plans and technical secrets. Refuse analysis saved his company millions of dollars in research and purchases of supplies at lower prices.[55]

71. FOREIGN HUMAN RESOURCES

Certain countries do not have trade secret protection laws effectively shielding the owner's proprietary rights. That means that it is legal, although perhaps immoral by Western standards, to buy/sell or otherwise obtain secret technical information from company employees or their liaisons. The Third World and Far East countries still do not have national espionage laws providing for punishment of foreign agents and state secrets' purveyors.

Illustration of foreign law ineffectiveness:

Four Japanese government employees, who gave away secret data on American F-16 and AWACS planes manufactured under license in Japan, were charged only with theft and dealing in stolen goods. The public employees were penalized by a $200.00 fine and a year in jail. That "severity" provided under the Japan's civil service code for peddling national secrets is not commensurate with the value of stolen goods and damage done to the product or method owner.[56]

Lack of serious penalties leads to disastrous financial losses resulting from illegal conveyance of goods.

Illustration of an illegal sale aftermath:

In 1982, Toshiba Machine Company, Ltd. sold the former Soviet Union four highly advanced milling machines through a trading company named C. Itoh & Co. A Norwegian Company, Kongsberg Trade Company, sold the Soviets four computer driven numerical controllers for guiding cutters of the Toshiba mills. The technology worth $21 million dollars was used to mill submarine propellers with such precision that Soviet submarines reduced their noise level almost tenfold.

The United States then had to spend about $30 million for research and development of a new tracking gear in order to detect the silenced Soviet submarines. The penalty for violation of Japan's Foreign Exchange Control Law and export regulations of COCOM (Coordination Committee on Multilateral Export controls monitoring sales of high-tech equipment to Communist countries): a one-year ban on Toshiba Machine Co. (a subsidiary of Toshiba Corp.) sales to Communist countries and a three-month ban on C. Itoh's sales.[57]

72. INSIDE INFORMATION

Inside information, i.e., information not known to the general public but only to a selected group of company employees and owners, has a tremendous value. For example, a securities firm, brokerage house or any financial institution may learn that a company became the target of a takeover bid. Although many investment and commercial bankers, stock traders, lawyers, journalists, and arbitragers routinely exchange such vital information, trading on such inside information is illegal.

As reported in the *Wall Street Journal*, May 15, 1986, an investment banker, Dennis B. Levine (a managing director in the merger and acquisitions department of a Wall Street firm Drexel Burnham & Lambert, Inc.), made about $12.6 million within five years by trading on inside information (about Jewel Co. and Textron Corp. stock). The example simply illustrates the value of such information collection means.

So called "inside information" may be gathered through observation of certain events, such as jet flights and meeting locations of executives, publicly registered stock purchases by insiders, and so forth. Inside information may be learned fortuitously.

Illustration:

One may overhear a business takeover plan in a public washroom. It would be legal to profit from a stock transaction based on such an event. It is also legal to deduct the inside information from legal and business documents given to a printer, binder, or other handler of information, who does not have a fiduciary (trust and confidence) relationship with the subject company, and who may use it for personal gain.

An employee may not use nonpublic company information for personal benefit, directly or indirectly. But if the insider did not benefit from tipping an outsider, who also personally did not benefit from the tip, the insider is not liable under the securities fraud laws.

73. PHOTO/VIDEO/AUDIO RECORDING

Documents, objects, people, equipment, performances may be memorialized through miniature audio and video recorders. Such recorders and cameras can be embodied in a lipstick, watch, car antenna, frame of sunglasses, cigarette lighter, cigarette pack, pen, book, clock and fire extinguisher.[58]

People's activity (extortion, lovemaking, transferring objects, assembling a product) and equipment operation are amenable to video recording. Conspicuous and hidden cameras are used to monitor medical and intelligence gathering operations, flow of people and their activity in buildings, stores, banks, manufacturing and design facilities, private and government investigations, court related proceedings and meetings.

74. INTERNET

One of the best corporate intelligence gathering tools is the Internet. It is cheap, quick, and absolutely legal. One may tap into the websites of competitors through the global computer network (the World Wide Web) and conduct online research ranging from the new product features and release date to acquisition and merger news.

The following is a list of Internet search engines (directories) and databases which may be helpful in gathering business data:

(1) ALTA VISTA (http://www.altavista.com): one of the best search engines on the Internet (more than 6 milliion Websites and 30,000,000 pages in its index and expanding daily) using quotations in order to get the optimum number of hits and including Usenet;

(2) INFOSEEK (http://www.infoseek.com): becoming one of the largest Web's directories, comprising Usenet (exchange message service) for reviewing the online chat between the newsgroups (universities and private companies), and using quotations, specific questions and capitalized names for searching the sites;

(3) ICEBREAKER (http://www.icemfg.com/icemfg): "data mining consultancy" (self-description) giving advice on gathering competitive intelligence;

(4) YAHOO (http://www.yahoo.com): a huge search engine including numerous fact-filled business sites;

(5) NATIONAL ASSOCIATION FOR THE SELF-EMPLOYED (NASE) (http://selfemployed.nase.org/NASE/info.html): legislative issues, business management tips, has a list of more than 300,000 members;

(6) SOCIETY OF COMPETITIVE INTELLIGENCE PROFESSIONALS (http://www.scip.org): useful tips for online sleuths;

(7) INDUSTRY.NET (http://www.industry.net): more than 4,000 business centers nesting self-profiled businesses and their products, daily newspaper, job bulletin, requests for customers and suppliers;

(8) ONLINE SECURITY (http://www.securityonline.com): information on Internet security.

(9) U.S. SMALL BUSINESS ADMINISTRATION (http://www.sba.gov): SBA source directory including financial assistance programs;

(10) SMALL BUSINESS ADVANCEMENT NATIONAL CENTER (http://www.sbaer.uca.edu/sbaer/databases/index.html): reports on international businesses, links to more than 30 industries;

(11) HOTELS & TRAVEL ON THE NET (http://www.hotelstravel.com): listing of hotels and travel-connected data, such as political activity in many countries, foreign country topography, ticketing and accomodation information;

(12) SECURITY MANAGEMENT ONLINE (http://www.securitymanagement.com): security information, overviews, bibliography of books, reports on campus and other facility security, crime statistics, commercial encryption products and export-connected enryption matters;

(13) STARTING POINT (http://www.stpt.com/refer.html): commercial directories;

(14) COMPETITIVE INTELLIGENCE (http://www.fuld.com): commercial data on company resources;

(15) AMERICAN SOCIETY FOR INDUSTRIAL SECURITY (http://www.asisonline.org): an international organization with more than 28,000 members worldwide; security-related information such as electronic countermeasures, investigations, deception detection and loss prevention, etc.;

(16) U.S. CENSUS BUREAU (http://www.census.gov): demographic facts (ethnic market size and location, news on population, economic and geographic data);

(17) PROFNET (http://www.vyne.com/profnet): experts in different fields;

(18) SUPERINTENDENT OF DOCUMENTS (http://www.access.gpo.gov/su_docs): official government documents, including Code of Federal Regulations, Congressional Record, Monthly Catalog of U.S. Government Publications and Federal Register;

(19) FEDERAL BULLETIN BOARD (http://fedbbs.access.gpo.gov): more than 7,000 files from 25-plus agencies and organizations from all three branches of the Federal Government;

(20) DENVICA-MALL ONLINE (http://www.denvica-mall.com): information emporium including the DENVICA 24-hour legal information bureau (1-900-680-6060), books (such as *How to pass exams on any subject*, *"Attorney's work-product: Vital legal information digest,"* etc.), seminars on business information protection, carry-on data products, and legal services related to economic counterespionage and trade secret safeguarding.

Tapping into the bulletin boards on the Net, news clips, databases, paying online sleuths and consultants and other electronic swathing, will generate lots of useful data on competitors, clients and suppliers.

75. CONSULATES

Each country tries to promote its businesses, products and services abroad. A consulate is an avanpost and avangard of every country abroad. Consulates maintain commercial databases about their country's businesses, trade shows, and so on. It is a duty of consulate representatives to provide information about companies and firms in their country. Consulates may put a foreigner in touch with any enterprise in their country, give a list of requested companies, or answer any question about the rules, statistics and procedures in their country, quickly and free of charge.

76. SPOUSES AND LOVERS

There are very few people who can totally block their spouses or lovers from "shop talk," such as discussion about co-workers, forthcoming events or business projects. "Pillow talks" and daily conversations about social functions, vacationing, health club or participation in sport activities, such as tennis or golf, elicit lots of inside information. That information may be picked up by "friends," hairdressers, manicurists, sport or social club partners communicating with the targets' spouses and lovers. Such indirect data collection is sometimes easier to accomplish than directly through the targets themselves.

77. CLEANING PERSONNEL

A janitorial worker cleaning hotel rooms, design studios, manufacturing facilities, offices and laboratories is left without supervision while working at night. Foreign intelligence agencies routinely use house-keeping and cleaning personnel to copy and photograph documents left in the hotel rooms, or copy the computer files onto diskettes from a running laptop computer. Even documents and items kept in a safe deposit box in a foreign hotel are not immune to review by intelligence agencies in that country.

78. INTERPRETERS

Interpreters, also doubling as tour guides, listen to business conversations between the negotiation team members. Interpreters report about the details of these discussions, and any other information they may have learned, to their employers.

79. PRIVATE INVESTIGATORS

Private detectives may ascertain the target's financial, romantic, medical, technical and social background. Such investigators, using their contacts with Interpol, FBI, state police and other governmental agencies, may observe, note, copy, videotape and photograph records, people and transactions. They will also testify in court about everything they discover. Some private investigators have contacts throughout the world.

There are many other ways to acquire competitors' intellectual property, such as pretext telephone calls, tasking foreign students and employees in a target country, corporate mergers and acquisitions, using front companies to fulfill classified contracts, and sponsoring technical or scientific research. These techniques are explored in seminars mentioned in PART 8 of this book.

PART 3

LOSSES OF PROPRIETARY DATA

In early 1996, FBI director Louis Freh warned Congress about a growing threat to national security because many countries are involved in economic espionage against U.S. companies. He said that at least twenty-three countries are engaged in industrial espionage in the United States and that about four hundred cases have been investigated since the Economic Counterintelligence Program was initiated in 1994. An additional three-hundred cases were investigated in 1996.[1]

Senator Arlen Specter (R.-Pa) said that at least fifty-one (51) nations, including Germany, Russia, Israel, France, Japan and China are involved in the espionage activities against U.S. companies. He stated that "U.S. businesses are losing 100 billion dollars a year because of foreign spying. Job losses are estimated to be over 6 million in this decade alone due to economic espionage."[2]

Business secrets have been stolen from time immemorial. Spying is the second oldest profession in the world. The secret-gathering business, encompassing research breakthroughs, marketing data, customer lists, even cooking methods and so forth, is a booming business. Business losses are not limited to sales or services taken away by technology pirates. The losses accumulate in many ways.

Losses resulting from commercial espionage comprise:

(1) Research and development cost. Research and development costs dramatically exceed the cost of designing around or copying a complex product. For instance, it is about a hundred times cheaper to copy a family of microprocessor chips than to develop them.[3]

Consequently, the product developer may be forced out of business by the competition which improperly "copied" the product and put it on the market with significantly lower prices. The original developer, burdened with the expensive research and development cost and unable to match the competitors' prices, loses its market share due to a product price (cost) differential.

(2) Loss of reputation. A manufacturer's reputation for reliability and quality is undermined if a bad counterfeit product bears the manufacturer's name. Loss of reputation results in loss of business because fewer purchasers will venture to acquire bad products.

(3) Litigation Cost. Emotionally and financially taxing lawsuits filed by the aggrieved product owners against trade secret thieves may be lost due to some legal technicalities. Litigation cost may be prohibitive and damages may be irreparable. In other words, a lawsuit victory may not justify all litigation expenses (which have to be added to the product cost) and achieve the intended objectives.

Illustration:

A lawsuit filed by the original designer resulted in a judgment against a foreign counterfeit product manufacturer in an American court. That manufacturer declares bankruptcy or dissolves a corporation so as to make collection on or enforcement of the judgment impossible. On top of this, the manufacturer reopens its operation under a different name and as another legal entity.

(4) Brain drain. Departure of the company's key employees caused by a competitor's "brain raid" or en masse exodus of employees may slow down the design and production of existing and future products. Besides the issue of data loss, such loss of employees simply cripples the company's ability to generate new products or service old ones in a timely fashion, and consequently makes the company non-competitive.

(5) Lead time. A competitor may have a lead time advantage by being first on the market with a product based on a purloined design.

PART 4

SAFEGUARDING PROPRIETARY INFORMATION

Now you know how information may be misappropriated or legally acquired. Knowledge of information loss and leak sources helps in the designing economic espionage countermeasures. This chapter delineates countermeasure system elements and instructions. The discussed system components demonstrate only a few measures which should be undertaken by a business enterprise.

A. RISK MANAGEMENT AND STRATEGIC PLANNING

Each proprietor of know-how, trade secrets, art works or other kinds of intellectual property must design and implement a property protection system in order to avoid revenue losses. Such a system starts by developing a plan and acsertaining who will do what and how.

A corporate strategic plan must be prepared by attorneys and managers of all departments since information loss may take place through any segment of the business. The plan should establish procedures to be followed routinely and in case of an emergency (contingency plans).

An information security committee or unit (including attorneys, security experts, and managers) should be set up for monitoring competitors' products, literature, technical and marketing activities; and for providing the senior management with its opinions (reports) concerning corporate and product development strategies.

The unit's responsibilities include:

(1) overseeing the release of their own secret information to the public, their employees, and to private companies through public statements, negotiation, bidding, announcements, sales and promotional materials, and presentations at the shows and conferences;

(2) identifying the company's proprietary data and setting forth security levels with respective trade secret protection measures;

(3) collecting competitors' corporate intelligence by gathering public records of competitors' stock ownership, contracts, announcements, patents, scientific publications and research presentations; attending trade shows and questioning competitors' salespeople and customers; and using other techniques discussed in this book;

(4) in case of international trade activity, assessing conflicts of laws, political, social and economic systems between the United States and foreign countries;

(5) creating personal profiles on important businessmen (potential enemies, business brokers or friends), scientists, political figures, and their families (such information may help the company to determine whom and how to hire, criticize, support, use, or leave alone);

(6) monitoring employees' and other parties' intelligence gathering activities and breaches of security procedures;

(7) issuing a manual prescribing (for all employees) security measures and evacuation plans in case of any disaster, such as fire, terrorist attacks, executive's kidnapping, or power failure;

(8) designating employees or hire security officers to police the implementation of the security procedures;

(9) supervising intracompany audits of documents, blueprints, samples, films and other proprietary material given to nonemployees for evaluation, which should be accounted for at regular intervals, say every six months.

Illustration of the unit's assignment or routine report:

A report may state that briberies, division of markets, and copying of proprietary products may be a normal modus operandi in the targeted foreign markets (countries). However, U.S. companies following these practices would run afoul of the U.S. antitrust and intellectual property protection laws. This opinion will help the senior management to assess the risks and benefits associated with the anticipated transactions and investment orientation.

Many U.S. companies, such as Schaumburg-based electronics giant Motorola, Inc., FMC Corporation (manufacturer of industrial chemicals, machinery and M-3 Bradley Fighting Vehicle) and Rockford-based Sundstrand Corp. (aerospace equipment producer), have set up their own intelligence/security units.[1]

B. INDUSTRIAL SECURITY AND COUNTERESPIONAGE METHODS

Industrial security measures are universal in their nature. However, they must be tailored to fit each business. What is appropriate for a bank may not be appropriate for a chemical concern. But the knowledge of protection methods will help a business in designing a defense program. The suggested industrial security steps are outlined in this section.

1. INFORMATION DISSEMINATION LIMITATIONS

Sensitive information should be disclosed to employees on a need-to-know basis with an attendant admonition to keep them secret. Broad exposure of confidential information may gain the trust and cooperation of employees but may hurt the business.

Illustration:

A salesperson learned from the company memorandum about a forthcoming price discount and then mentioned this to a customer. The customer conveyed this information to a competitor who immediately matched the forthcoming discount. Thus, the advantage of the discount surprise was negated.[2]

Illustrations of sensitive information which should not be divulged broadly, particularly in writing:

(1) salaries of employees;

(2) company's financial status before it becomes public;

(3) acquisition, merger or company's sale negotiations;

(4) new product specifications and pricing plans.

2. CLASSIFIED DOCUMENT STORAGE

Important confidential documents should be numbered, imprinted with each document recipient's name, dated, identified on a list of document recipients, and kept in one place along with said list. A legend on a title page should specify the return date of that copy and expressly forbid copying or circulating the document. Confidential material must be accounted for at all times. Minutes of all meetings with non-employees must be recorded. Computer files of certain classified documents must be erased upon printing of a hard copy. Electronically stored documents must be encrypted and kept in directories accessible to authorized personnel only.

3. PERSONNEL SCRUTINY

The meticulous analysis of the behavior of a business' personnel is a continuous process for the employer. In order to discover employees who are vulnerable to blackmail or other unsavory recruitment methods, one needs to conduct periodic lie detector and voluntary drug tests, check credit reports to find out who is experiencing financial difficulty, even hire private detectives if necessary. Bankruptcy may be considered as one of the grounds for employee's termination (for certain job categories). One should make these tests a condition of employment.

A luxurious way of life (in comparison to similarly situated employees) may uncover an employee with a suspicious source of income.

Illustration of a security lapse:

The wife of a naval petty officer Terry Whitworth, who sold ciphers and codes to the Soviets for thousands of dollars, picked him up in a Rolls-Royce and spent at one time about $1,600 on lingerie. Security personnel should have realized that a petty officer's salary cannot accomodate such luxury.

4. EXIT INTERVIEW

Ask the departing employee what company materials she took from the company's premises and what her new position will be. Tell the employee that the company's proprietary information is the company's valuable property and the employees have perpetual obligation to keep product information and trade secret confidential even if she retains some of this information in her memory.

The company's uncompromising attitude toward the prosecution of employees violating their fiduciary and contractual obligations must be reflected in the exit interview. The employee has to be reminded about her continuous obligations with respect to documentation of inventions and patent applications. The departing employee should sign a nondisclosure agreement covering particular trade secrets and projects, which the employee took part in and learned about, as identified by the employee's supervisors.

5. WASTE AND DOCUMENT DISPOSAL

Destruction devices must be provided for laboratory samples, printer's proofs of contract and business proposal drafts, new product design drafts, marketing plans and promotional literature, waste paper, rejects, computer diskettes, drawings and trash. Garbage cans located near copiers should be supplemented with paper shredders. A record of the destruction of documents or the retrieval of given-for-evaluation sensitive documents must be maintained.

The destruction and declassification of documents should be routine and systematic. The most sensitive documents should be destroyed immediately after reading them. All memoranda, correspondence and similar documents, except research and statistical data and income tax related materials, should be systematically destroyed after six months storage or some other appropriate interval.

For short-lived memoranda, one may use a commercially available roller ball-point pen with ink disappearing a few hours after application. The ink invented by a Russian secret service and reverse engineered by Americans may be purchased through mail-order magazines. Use water soluble "paper" for recording extremely sensitive information which should be destroyed quickly (dissolution occurs within a few seconds in warm water). The water soluble material looks and behaves like a paper but in fact it is made from sodium barboxy methyl cellulose, wood fibers (for tearing purposes) and calcium carbohydrate (for opacity). This "paper" is popular with mob bookmakers, the Pentagon (after the USS Pueblo secret documents' capture by North Koreans in 1968), and intelligence services in NATO countries.[3]

Systematic destruction of intracompany documents made pursuant to a company policy may even help in product liability and other lawsuits filed against the company.

6. ELECTRONIC AND INTEROFFICE MAIL

Each E-mail statement is subject to discovery in lawsuits. These statements may contain trade secret information or admissions against own interest about competitors' products. There is no privacy in electronic communications. Messages can be monitored by employers, intercepted by outsiders, disclosed for litigation purposes, or received by unintended recipients.

Electronic mail messages are permanently saved either on the computer network or Internet servers (for backup or achival purposes), unless and until each recipient's directory and the servers are purged. Such permanent record may expose the employer to legal liability arising from sexual harassment, discrimination, trade secret, patent and copyright infringement claims. Seemingly innocent messages or jokes may cost the employer millions of dollars in penalties and judgments. Critical business data may be lost through either E-mail eavesdropping, misaddressing, or excessive dissemination.

Illustration of E-mail message security measures:

(1) give each employee a manual describing the employer's computer security policy and (a) emphasizing the record creating and legal ramification effect of each E-mail message; (b) prohibiting the use of offensive language, jokes, personal, political, advertising or copyrighted material;

(2) instruct employees to use communication codes in lieu of descriptive terms, if appropriate;

(3) verify the recipient's address prior to sending the E-mail since the message may go to the unintended group of users;

(4) include in an employment agreement provisions stating that the E-mail system and computer software belong to the employer, employee agrees that all electronic communications will be monitored by the employer, and no defamatory, discriminating, personal, trade secret disclosing or copyright infringement (video images, or audio material, or pictures, which belong to other parties) statement shall be made in the E-mail messages;

(5) review E-mail going to outsiders;

(6) reports of the security violations must promptly investigated and acted on by the employer;

(7) communications with attorneys must bear a warning "Attorney-Client Privileged" on each page;

(8) E-mail messages of any kind and, particularly messages containing trade secret or the unauthorized personal, offensive, or copyrighted material, should be deleted as soon as practically possible;

(9) encrypt E-mail communications whenever and wherever possible.

Here are a few of internal mail precautions: labeling envelopes with cautionary legends, changing delivery methods, and return or destruction of a document upon review. Interoffice or external mail should not bear any sign of secrecy classification on the outer envelopes and should be sealed with a tape signed over by the addressor.

7. PROTECTION OF FACILITIES

The security system should utilize a combination of steps, such as employing guards, securing document safes to concrete walls or floor, conducting camera surveillance, installing remote-controlled door locks, camouflaging the plant and products, and so forth.

Illustrations of security devices:

Motion detectors sensing people passing through the door in the disallowed directions and triggering door locking devices, beepers identifying a location of such locking door on security officer's screen, self-lockable one-way revolving doors, employee picture badges (with recorded identification data) which are screened by readers mounted at the doors, alarm systems, and fake alarm stickers in places where one may not easily discover that the systems are not in existence (on columns, walls, doors).

In lieu of security guards, access to segregated areas may be controlled by optical turnstiles combining infrared technology and non-contact card readers. A closed circuit television (CCTV) system may control access to segregated areas via access booths with overhead and side scan image of a person entering the booth. Biometric recognition devices restrict access by comparing the user's physical characteristics (fingerprints, palm outline and creases, wrist and retinal vein patterns, signature, ear shape, facial elements, electrocardiogram, finger length, hand geometry, keyboard striking rhythm, gait and voice) with the electronically stored files or the card data. In the future, signature dynamics devices will authenticate the identity of the user by examining speed, appearance and rhythm of the user's signature writing.

8. VISITORS

Allow visits by appointment only and request that all visitors sign a non-disclosure agreement, including the repairmen. Visitors should indicate in a log, maintained at the security or front desk, their name, address, "in" and "out" time, name of the employee expecting them, and purpose of the visit. The company employees must meet visitors in a lobby and then take them to a meeting place.

Visitors should never be left alone, because they can read papers spread on the office desks and notices posted on the boards, leave "bugs," misrepresent their identity to other employees, steal documents and things. Visitors' ID cards (color coded and worn on the neck chains or clipped to the clothing) can be issued in duplicates and collected by the security guards or receptionists, who also should collect, initial and date the visitors' business cards. Visitor ID cards must be disposed of or be self-degradable so as no one could use them again.

The employee must record information which was disclosed to visitors, for example, by writing a memorandum to file, or sending a "thank-you" letter also stating what was discussed at the meeting, or a mutual understanding confirmation letter to that visitor.

Facility tours for the public should be avoided. Tours conducted by the employees must be routed through selected areas only and while maintaining a substantial distance between the observers and protectible equipment or documents. Employees should not discuss any business matters (not even disclose titles and names of other employees) with unescorted visitors. Some areas must be completely off limits to visitors.

No audio or video images of the plant or laboratory/research facility interior, even as a background, should be recorded by any non-employee or employee without written authorization by a designated company executive. Snapshots of a birthday party or individual employees should not be allowed in the areas where bulletin boards with office notices are located, product prototypes or CAD-CAM monitors displaying the latest designs are visible.

9. DIVISION OF PROPRIETARY INFORMATION

Divide product formula into independent components, disguise product development steps, and code product ingredients or documents.

Ilustration:

Component isolation (information segregation) is exemplified in Colonel Sander's handling of a special seasoning formula for Kentucky Fried Chicken (KFC) which is kept secret by dividing the secret blending process between two licensees. Each of these licensees knows only its portion of the formula and blending system for it. One of these licensees mixes together two blended components and sells the complete seasoning to distributors or retail operators. Both companies (Strange and Sexton) signed secrecy agreements with the KFC Corporation. These companies manufactured and sold the secret seasoning for 25 years and no other chicken spice supplier could sell its seasoning to KFC franchisees. Each franchisee signed a contract to buy only the KFC coating mix. Such exclusive supply arrangement precludes franchisees from reaching other suppliers on the market and forces the franchisee to maintain the confidentiality of the franchisor's trade secrets.[4]

10. SCRAMBLING OF COMMUNICATIONS

Encrypt telephone, facsimile, satellite and computer data transmission messages using off-the shelf encryption software and stationary or portable encoders which may be carried in the attache cases. Key personnel, ad hoc committee or negotiating teams (during the negotiation talks, data evaluation and advance purchase plan meetings), may use encrypted telephones for secure phone calls which can "talk" to normal telephones. Once contact is established, the switch on the phone transfers it into a coded mode and termination of a call reverts it to the normal code. There are cordless, cellular and other types of telephones which automatically scramble telephone communications.

11. COMPUTER SYSTEM SAFEGUARDS.

The ease by which computer-based data can be illegally obtained at almost no risk make computers the favorite target of information thieves. Computer protection systems should have user restrictions which identify a person or entity seeking access to a computer system by personalized digital signatures and passwords. There are also restrictions on computer system resources rather than on users.

Illustrations of computer security measures:

(1) implant safeguards into computer programs, such as instructions to erase, shutdown the system, and leave a trail of breach of security markers which may be triggered by an unauthorized attempt to connect to the system;

(2) security "moles" embedded into a program help to prove copying of the information, such as harmless errors, logic bombs, false codes or initials, copyright notices invisible on the screen during the execution of the misappropriated program;

(3) install "screen savers" (programs that either blank out the screen or switch the display to cartoons and moving objects upon predetermined intervals in user's activity) with passwords (different than log-in passwords) and voice recognition algorithms allowing only the authorized user to re-start the interrupted activity;

(4) lock the doors and lock up computers, turn monitors away from the passages used by visitors, place partitions blocking the monitors from the passing public;

(5) set up "antivirus" (a virus is a program which reproduces itself in another program, to erase data and damage the software) measures, such as regular data backups, waiting for a few weeks prior to downloading the shareware into your system, installing the antivirus software which must be constantly updated (as new virus programs are born almost every week) by obtaining the latest version thereof through the Internet or mail;

(6) implement an "electronic firewall" comprising encryption systems to scramble and de-scramble messages and files, user authentication (credit card size) devices equipped with a computer chip generating a random 6 to 10 number code each   minute, and E-mail security management products.

12. MAKING ERRORS

Make typographical or other harmless but inconspicuous mistakes in the software or documents which would help to prove copying of the material in court proceedings. For example, mapmakers often put the names of non-existent small towns on highway or state maps for this purpose.

13. REVERSE ENGINEERING COUNTERMEASURES

To prevent reverse engineering of a leased or sold product, rig it with mechanical (for instance, plastic or lead wrapping) encasing, or chemical (such as odor emitting gas capsules breakable by product tampering) detectors. A lead sheet around the product or product component will block the X-raying of its interior. Install product destructing, damaging or discoloring devices which are activated by tampering.

14. PRE-EMPLOYMENT SCREENING

The personnel department should verify awards, addresses (by sending the company printed material to the applicant's address using return-receipt mail), reasons for joining and discharging from the army, prior employment (looking for conflicting dates and unexplained gaps in employment history), license and diploma issuance, previous employment agreements, business references. They should also conduct drug and psychological testing (for certain positions).

Graphology (the study of handwriting) may be one of predictors of the new hire character traits. A handwriting analysis may be used to determine an employee's suitability for a promotion, ego drive, risk aversion, confidence and impatience. The analysis takes into consideration space, size, movement, rhythm, and slant of the letters.

No photocopies of documents should be acceptable. Ask to bring the originals for copying on site. Job applicants have to sign "a release of data" form authorizing any company, educational institution or service to release information (without any liability) as to the applicant's background to the new employer.

Illustration of negligent screening:

A gigantic defense contractor with an extensive security system inadequately investigated the job applicants and hired an ex-convict and high school dropout as an engineer in its most secret program.[5]

15. PRE-EMPLOYMENT INTERVIEWS

Before the commencement of employment, all employees must sign employment agreements identifying employee's inventions and ideas made prior to the subject employment. These inventions will be excluded from the future employment-related inventions. The employees should also disclose and assign to their employers "all inventions, discoveries or developments" after the employment commencement. This is necessary to cover both patented inventions and trade secrets made during the employment and one year thereafter, unless such ideas or inventions do not relate to the company's business.[5]

As a necessary part of a pre-employment interview, the interviewer should find out :

- Existence, custody and terms of nondisclosure, noncompetition and employment agreements signed with previous employers.
- Reason for leaving the former employer(s).
- Identity of projects the applicant was involved in and in what

capacity.

The purpose of these inquiries is to make sure that there is no intent to steal the competitor's or your company's (an applicant can be a spy) trade secrets, to avoid a potential lawsuit and to find the proper placement within the organization for the applicant.

16. COMMUNICATION CODES

Sensitive information should not be discussed, whether in private (even with a relative or a friend) or in public, outside the company. No discussions among the members of a negotiating team should be conducted outside the company (subject to the above delineated rules of conduct) with respect to the sensitive information. The parties, subject matter, contractors, suppliers, technology, and contract terms (volume, location, capacity, profit margin, royalty and price) should be coded in advance. The team members should practice communication code terms and speak the sign language which can be used for certain occasions.

Illustration of a communication code:

One of the Chicago street gangs called El Rukn developed a secret communication code to discuss their business: drug dealing. The code was based on assignment of words to numbers, delivery terms, events, money and products. The following is a partial list of coded terms used by the gang members:

"Perfect" means "marijuana";
"Race car" or "brewery" means "cocaine";
"Love" means one, 100 or 1,000;
"Love, truth" means two, 200 or 2,000;
"Justice" means weapon.
"Love, truth, peace, freedom, four grapes and a half grape" means $445.

"We can get a calendar for possession of perfect" means "We can get one year in prison for possession of marijuana".

"The brewery will not be in manifest" means "The cocaine will not be delivered".[7]

This simple code was very effective. The police were only able to break it with the help of former gang members.

Illustration of another type of communication code:

Air traffic controllers identify airlines by nicknames, such as Cactus for American West airline, Blackjack for Atlantic World Airways, Speedbird for British Airways, Clipper for Pan Am, Critter for Valujet, Manatee for AirTran, and Aussie for Royal Australian Air Force.[8]

17. BOGUS REPORTS

Reports containing distorted facts may be periodically given to a selected group of people. If there is any leak of such facts, it would be easier to pin down the source of such a leak. It is one type of a litmus test of the employees' ability to keep the information confidential.

18. TRADE SHOWS

Taking pictures of the displayed equipment and product at the trade shows may be made only upon consent of the company's representatives. Salesmen must be instructed what to say and what not to say to all non-employees about the product, its development, costs and marketing plans. Socializing rules, reverse engineering methods, blackmail techniques should be explained to the marketing and sales personnel representing the company at the trade show. Exhibit protection measures have to be developed and implemented.

19. REJECTS

One avenue for industrial espionage is the acquisition (legal and illegal) of rejects which did not pass the quality control inspection but which could disclose the structure and composition of the product. Therefore, rejects should be always accounted for and destroyed, or damaged beyond "recognition" to hamper the reverse engineering of the product.

20. ELECTRONIC SURVEILLANCE COUNTERMEASURES

Window and wall vibrations reflect indoor conversations. Voice-generated vibrations, which can be picked up by a laser device from the windows. Computer signals may be picked up by signal receiving and converting equipment, and other devices which may even record conversations through the wall.

Illustrations of simple countermeasures which may neutralize some surveillance contraptions:

(1) background music, radio or TV broadcast during important conversations and meetings;

(2) placing aluminum strips on windows (a very old technique);

(3) placing sound-generating devices or micro speakers on windows;

(4) installing windows with bulges distorting reflected signals;

(5) setting up phone tap defeating devices and countersurveillance equipment neutralizing dropout relays, infinity and free running transmitters, voice activated recorders and room audio bugs;

(6) conducting electronic "sweeping" for the detection of "bugs" (micro transmitters) at all facilities where sensitive information may be discussed; and

(7) installing computer data encryption equipment eliminating electronic compromise of computer signals picked up by Van Eck eavesdropping devices (receiving computer-generated electromagnetic pulses from about a mile away as these signals travel like radio waves).

Countersurveillance experts help to select and install the appropriate equipment throughout the facilities.

C. LEGAL PROTECTION OF INTELLECTUAL PROPERTY

Besides physical or tangible security measures, including installation of alarms, trap doors, and paper shredders, designed to protect the facilities and personal property of the owner, one must also set forth espionage countermeasures including legal protection of the intangible business assets. Intellectual property means trade secrets, patents, know-how, trademarks, trade names, service marks and copyrights. Intellectual property is a very valuable intangible asset. One needs to distinguish what belongs to the general public (public domain) and what is proprietary, to wit, belongs to the inventor or business owner and needs to be protected. The following is a discussion of legal protection avenues which each business may use for shielding proprietary business data from pilferage and even business demise.

1. NEGOTIATIONS

Business negotiations should be conducted with great caution, so as not to disclose more information than is necessary for the consummation of a deal. A presentation ought to concentrate on what an article or system does, rather than how it does it. A cardinal negotiation rule: "Never volunteer unrequested and needless information." Prepare an outline of what should be and should not be discussed during the negotiations.

Illustrations of basic negotiation rules:

(1) know your own costs, minimum profit margins, delivery and volume capabilities, bottom line terms and negotiation strategy prior to entering into any negotiation discussion;

(2) show the opponents the benefits which would result from the proposed deal;

(3) learn about the negotiators (style, traits, technical and personal background);

(4) create, practice and use intracompany communication codes for identification of products, volumes, deadlines, parties, locations and contract terms;

(5) learn about the people who may authorize the deal and seek meetings with them;

(6) meet at a neutral place, thereby alleviating fears of eavesdropping and improving the spirit of cooperation;

(7) know the opponent's deadline because stress and respective concessions usually increase when the deadline is approaching;

(8) watch for the opponent's body language, listen attentively and without interrupting the speaker, watch for hugs, shoulder pats, use of first name, maintain eye contact, control own and observe the opponent's facial expressions;

(9) do not discuss the offered terms with the team members near or in the presence of the opponents, service personnel, or in the opponent's offices, elevators, or a foreign hotel room;

(10) disclose to the opponent what the system or product would do but not how it would do that, or in other words, a minimum of technical data should be revealed, particularly at the initial deal negotiation.

(11) technical details ought to be kept secret, if possible, or at least to be disclosed only after signing the contract;

(12) use silence as a powerful negotiation tool because silence makes the opponent uneasy;

(13) do not keep secret documents in a hotel safe which local intelligence services may easily access, but rather mail them to yourself (via international couriers or express mail services) or keep them at the U.S. embassy; and

(14) do not discuss sensitive information in the presence of an interpreter provided by a foreign government or opposing parties.

2. SCREENING OF PUBLICATIONS AND PRESENTATIONS

Have attorneys devise a system of screening by attorneys of speeches and publications prepared by the research, engineering, public relations, and marketing personnel, and other employees being a privy to secret information. Pictures of production lines, security equipment, document shelters, as well as material specifications, tolerance criteria, manufacturing data or other information determined as being secret one, should be withdrawn from all documentation and sales literature prior to public disclosure and sales of the product. Training, operating and software manuals may be licensed. These or other legal limitations on disclosure and dissemination of the information create a legal distribution barrier.

Illustration of a trade secret being lost via sales literature:

Listing representative clients in the firm's advertising booklets subverted a businessman's claim of the customer list secrecy in litigation with a former employee who copied such a list.

3. CONFIDENTIAL DISCLOSURE AGREEMENTS

Employees with access to a secret process or equipment must sign a nondisclosure agreement. Each employee, independent contractor or consultant should sign an express agreement not to reveal business-related information to outsiders. The agreements should specify the projects and duration of agreements. Non-disclosure agreements alone may be sufficient trade secret protection measures.[9]

If a non-disclosure contract is not signed, but an employee knows that the information is deemed by the employer to be a trade secret, the commercial secret may be protected by court.[10] But one should not rely on the courts to provide adequate trade secret protection.

Confidential information developed by an employee may be used by the employee after termination of the employment if the nondisclosure agreement specifically excludes such information. Also, minor modifications of the known art (no research or experimentation was involved) will belong to the employee. Trade secrets should be defined broadly in the nondisclosure agreement and company's policy guide ought to be incorporated by reference for definition of specific employee obligations. Trade secret protection will not be vitiated by distribution of the sensitive information if such confidentiality agreements have been executed.

Illustration:

Data General Corporation gave out design drawings (maintenance diagrams) of its Nova 1200 computers to more that 6,000 people under the nondisclosure agreements without losing trade secret protection for the disclosed design.[11]

Conversely, avoid signing of nondisclosure agreements when negotiating with others in order not to impede your own technological development by tipping off the competition. Always disclose what your innovation is all about and what it can do, but not how it is designed or its secret components or technology.

4. NONCOMPETITION AGREEMENTS

All employees should sign noncompetition agreements restricting future competitive employment of an employee within certain territorial limits for a specified period of time. Such agreements should be signed before the commencement of employment, because signing after the commencement and without any new consideration provided by the employer may make such agreements unenforceable.

It is possible to sign these agreements during the employment. In order to avoid uncertainty, additional consideration should be given to the current employees at the time of signing the agreement. Consideration may be in the form an extended vacation plan, increased insurance coverage, a raise or stock bonus.

In some states, however, non-competition agreements are not enforceable, for example, in California, Florida and Michigan.[12] Non-competition agreements are broader than non-disclosure agreements, because "even in the best of good faith...an employee working for a competitor...can hardly prevent his knowledge of his former employer's confidential methods from showing up in his work."[13]

Therefore, a non-competition covenant avoids the issue of inevitable disclosure and consequent violation of the non-disclosure agreement.[14] A nondisclosure or confidentiality agreement may obviate the need for a noncompetition agreement.

One way to by-pass a noncompetition agreement is to offer the departing employee a consulting job with an attendant restriction not to work for a competitior while being employed by the company as a consultant. A company may even agree to pay ex-employees base salaries for a few years after the employment termination, if the agreement precludes similar employment.[15]

5. SUBMISSIONS TO GOVERNMENT

Mandatory disclosure laws require submission of information to the U.S. and state governments. Trade secrets may be learned by competitors from such disclosures through requests under the Freedom of Information Act or otherwise. Consequently, certain cautionary measures should be undertaken in order to minimize the exposure of know-how and proprietary information to the public.

Disclosed material protection may be carried out through warnings, precensored versions of the disclosure or legal loopholes. In order to protect the valuable data which must be submitted to the governmental agencies (such as Environmental Protection Agency, Food and Drug Administration, etc.), the following techniques may be undertaken:

(a) Submit to the government agency two sets of documents, one designated for public release (precensored) and the second one designated to meet the governmental agency's requirements (such as identity of ingredients, names of packets, etc.);

(b) Mark the requested documentation as "confidential proprietary information" with a request to submit to the company the names of the data requesters and information to be released to such requesters; and

(c) Label the documents containing proprietary information with prominently displayed notice "Disclosure exemption is requested under the Freedom of Information Act, 5 U.S.C. 552(b)(4)". Request exemption from the disclosure pursuant to the nine statutory exemptions listed in the Freedom of Information Act (FOIA).

Illustration of a disclosure avoidance (exemption) technique:

Under the National Defense Authorization Act for Fiscal Year 1997 (10 U.S.C. Sec. 2305 (g) and 41 U.S.C. Sec. 253b(m)), the FOIA Exemption 3 statutes have been amended to prohibit civilian and defense agencies from releasing contractor proposals, unless the proposal was actually set forth or incorporated into the contract entered between the agency and the offeror. The proposal means any technical, management, or cost proposal, submitted by any contractor in response to the requirements of a solicitation for a competitive proposal. Accordingly, such contractor proposals can now be legally protected from the disclosure to the public, and, consequently, to the competitors.

The above example demonstrates the use of the obscure statutory amendments (of the Freedom of Information Act through the National Defense Act) and shows that a careful analysis of the law and precedents may justify the disclosure exemption requests.

6. MARKING

When appropriate, place registered trademark and copyright notices on every product, product manual, service describing brochure, sales literature and other documents distributed to the public. Label every product with patent numbers for patents which cover the product features. Labeling gives notice to potential infringers and starts the period during which the infringement damages may be recovered. Note: If possible, delete all supplier identification and manufacturing code marks on each component of the assembled product prior to its sales to the public.

7. UNSOLICITED IDEA SUBMISSION

An original and unsolicited idea clearly described and submitted in confidence to a company, which commercially utilizes the same or similar idea, may trigger a lawsuit from an unhappy submitter. Almost every word of the preceding sentence is important because it incorporates court decisions concerning such submissions. For example, if the idea disclosed in confidence is not novel, no misappropriation liability will arise.[16]

The courts determine whether the unsolicited idea submitted to and implemented by the company is in fact a new and great idea by considering the following elements:

(a) The novelty of the idea (some degree of novelty is required).

(b) The concreteness of the idea (not merely a general idea, but a specific structure or steps in a new method).

(c) Exploitation (selling, distributing, using) of the idea by the recipient.

(d) Solicitation of the idea by the inventor or invention user.

(e) Confidentiality of disclosure of the idea to the company representatives.

(f) Contractual relationship between the parties (inventor and recipient/user of the invention).

Lawsuits with regard to misappropriation of unsolicited idea may uncover the company's secret marketing and product development plans as to this idea, drain company's resources on litigation and force to pay out undeserved compensation. Therefore, in order to avoid such lawsuits, a company should set up a preventive measure system.

Illustrations of such system components:

(1) All incoming mail associated with the unsolicited non-employee idea disclosures must go to a single source within the recipient's company. That source should be one or two non-technical employees (such as secretaries or receptionists) who would not be able to understand or use the submitted material.

(2) These non-technical employees should send to the idea submitter the standard confidential disclosure waivers which expressly state that no ideas will be considered until the submitter waives secrecy and confidentiality of the disclosure, and acceptance of such a submission for consideration purposes will not give rise to a contract.

(3) Only upon receipt of a waiver, these employees should send the disclosure to the technical personnel for evaluation.

(4) Keep a good record of the product development, so as to document an independent (of the submitted idea) development of the same idea.

(5) No other employee, particularly the technical personnel, should accept or even read unsolicited outsider suggestions.

8. NOTICE TO NEW EMPLOYER

Advise a new employer about your ex-employee's non-competition and secrecy agreements. Notice should be free from additional facts or explanations, which may be misinterpreted or used by the disgruntled ex-employee as a basis for a lawsuit. Conversely, upon hiring the competitor's employees, ask a job applicant about all previous employment agreements and verify the existence of such agreements by writing to the ex-employer.

These techniques may help your company to avoid a lawsuit claiming tortious interference with the employee's contractual relationship with their former employer, economic espionage, unjust enrichment and unfair competition based on misappropriation of ex-employer's labor, expenses and skill.

9. CONFLICT OF INTEREST

At least twice a year, employees should fill out a conflict-of-interest form identifying employee's business dealings and financial involvement with the employer's competitors, suppliers and customers. Such involvement ought to be cleared by the employee's superiors.

10. CUSTOMER LIST PROTECTION

A customer list is a protectable trade secret. In order to preserve the rights to that secret, one should undertake the following steps:

(a) divide the knowledge of the client's identity between the employees, i.e. only a segment of the client's list may become available to an employee servicing that segment of respective clients;

(b) attach proprietary legends to each copy of the client identity data;

(c) sign nondisclosure and confidentiality agreements with employees upon hiring them;

(d) remind employees about the penalties caused by violation of the company's security policy including prosecution for theft, industrial espionage and misappropriation of a customer list or other business secrets;

(e) remind the employees, throughout their employment (through notices, meetings, videos, educational seminars) and at the employment termination meeting, that the list is confidential.

The border line between proper and improper means of obtaining a customer list (business data collection) may not be clearly defined.

Illustration of a customer list loss:

Because the client names were known to two ex-employees (accountants) who started their own firm and the clients' addresses could be obtained from other sources, these employees did not steal trade secrets when they used the employer's card file, which contained such names and addresses, for mailing office and business-related announcements.[17]

11. PATENTS

In return for the required disclosure of the best mode of the invention to the public, the patentee obtains the right to exclude others from making, using or selling the patented invention for twenty years from the date of filing a patent application for a utility patent or fourteen years (from the date of issuance) for a design patent. This clear protection is particularly good for a proprietary product or method. A utility patent discloses the product, or structure, or process/method steps. A design patent protects the overall appearance of a structure without disclosing how it operates.

Patents create a formidable defense which may crush patent infringers with actual and even treble damages, post-infringement interest, attorney's fees, legal costs and a permanent injunction. For example, an owner of a patent on an O-ring seal for a drill bit was awarded more than $200 million for patent infringement.[10] Even less prosaic patented inventions brought multi-million dollar recoveries from patent infringers.

Patents may be used "offensively" by licensing of the patented item and swapping or cross-licensing the patents. Patents enhance a business resale value, offer an opportunity to exchange the technologies by cross-licensing, generate income through licensing or outright sale thereof, bolster a product's value, and even force a competitor (patent infringer) out of business.

Illustration of a business demise due to patent infringement:

After a 10-year patent infringement battle, Kodak was forced to end its instant camera business (4,500 people lost jobs, 16 million cameras made instantly obsolete) which generated about $200 million per year. More that seven years and $200 million in research and development were lost because Kodak infringed Polaroid's patents protecting its instant camera (which was introduced in 1972). The upshot of this story is that were it not for the effective protection of its product, Polaroid could have lost its competitive edge to a company which was almost ten times larger ($11 billion v. $1.3 billion in revenues).[19]

12. TRADE SECRETS

Trade secret may be defined as any formula, device or information used in a trade or business, which give the owner an advantage over competitors. It may be a chemical formula, tool, customers list, product specifications, marketing plans, bookkeeping or other office management method, a code for determining discounts, rebates or other price concessions, etc. (The Restatement of Torts, 1939). Novelty and invention are not requisites of a trade secret, but secrecy and absence of general knowledge in the trade or business, or public knowledge of the item, are. However, some originality is required.

Illustration:

Replacing vacuum tubes with transistors would not qualify for a trade secret, because it is not sufficiently original.[20]

According to The Restatement of Torts, Section 757, comment (b), at 6 (1939), the information is deemed to be a trade secret upon considering the following factors:

(a) the secret's novelty;

(b) whether the secret is a secret;

(c) proprietor's time, labor and money expended in development of the trade secret;

(d) continuous efforts to maintain the information secrecy within and outside proprietor's business;

(e) confidentiality of the relationship between the parties knowing the secret;

(f) the value to the trade secret owner and to the competition;

(g) difficulty of reverse engineering.

Trade secret protection is particularly advantageous for a production method, while patent protection is advantageous for a product made by that method. Many companies keep their secrets secret instead of patenting them.

Illustration:

Colonel Sander's seasoning mix for Kentucky Fried Chickens, perfume formulae, and Coca-Cola syrup (a secret since 1885) keep their value mainly due to the secrecy surrounding their ingredients and preparation process.

Trade secrets (e.g., a buyer's list, market research or sale force analysis) can be combined with patent protection. A license agreement involving both patents and trade secrets may oblige a licensee to pay royalties beyond the life of the licensed patents for the use of trade secrets but not for the use of the patented product or process. Therefore, different royalty rates may be allocated for licensed trade secrets and patents.

Trade secrets are valuable commodities which may be worth millions of dollars. These secrets may be lost through company's own disclosure to the public, reverse engineering and other means.

Illustration of a trade secret loss avenue:

The existence of the "Popeye's Inc." chicken chain ($300 million in annual sales) may be jeopardized if one of its franchisees prevails in a lawsuit involving the secret coating for chicken. If a franchisee's claim that his recipe was created by reverse engineering (by analyzing the recipe) is true, then "Popeye's" could lose more than $1 million spent in research and development of its recipe for Cajun-style chicken.[21]

In all trade secret misappropriation cases, the courts must determine whether an alleged trade secret is proprietary to the employer or merely a part of the employee's general knowledge and skill. Former employees may continue to enjoy their trade or vocation if the alleged secret information is general business information not proprietary to the employer.[22]

Information pertaining to single or transient business event is not qualified for trade secret protection, e.g. terms of a secret contract bid, salary of particular employees, security investments made or contemplated, announcement dates of a new product or plan, etc. Restatement of Torts, Sec. 757, comments (1939).

Trade secret protection is lost as soon as it becomes publicly available by publication (in a patent, advertising brochures, technical papers, a technology pooling agreement, a picture in the company's annual report, or a trade magazine article) or by sales in the open market, or can be ascertained by disassembling the product.[23]

Illustration of a commercial secret loss due to a company's own negligence:

Information (a customer list) stored on a disk that was sold together with a computer to a third party loses its trade secret protection.[24]

Trade secrets may be lost due to inadequate security measures. Trade secrets are considered misappropriated when they were (a) disclosed in confidence and then used in breach of that confidence; or (b) obtained by unlawful means. The adequacy of security measures for maintaining qualified (absolute secrecy is unnecessary) secrecy depends on circumstances. Trade secret security measures may create an impression or appearance of the extant secrecy and influence a judge or a jury that the sensitive information was in fact secret.

Non-public information, such as the availability of a business for acquisition, advice on acquisition, expansion opportunities, and finding such a business, do not qualify as a trade secret because such information is not used to run the business but is the product of the business. Any business, regardless of its size, needs to know what information must be protected from commercial espionage and inadvertent loss.

Proprietary information, which can be protected as trade secrets, may stem from a process, system or device for continuous use in business operations. The following is a partial list of such information and possible commercial secrets by category.

Technical Information

* Product ingredients, such as a chicken seasoning mix
* Blueprints
* Prototypes and concepts
* Software developed in-house
* Process equipment not shown to the general public
* Field test data
* Research results (e.g. oil deposit location calculation on the basis of a geophysical data)
* Engineering techniques (using screws in lieu of welds, stress reducing design).

Marketing Information

* License or contract terms (prices, suppliers, etc.)
* Customer list
* Advertisements and advertising campaigns
* Research data as to competitors' products, services and personnel
* Economic forecast for the company and the industry
* Agreement expiration date (knowledge of the insurance policy or

investment agreement expiration date allows the competition to more effectively solicit and take away business)
* Marketing plan and research (e.g. as to what advertising technique should be used for a particular business, to what company personnel such advertising should be addressed, the most beneficial time or territory for selling a product).

Business Operation

* Equipment and its exploitation efficiency
* Acquisitions and mergers
* Product delivery schedules
* Knowledge of lead times in component supply
* Collection of quotations
* Employee training methods
* Methods of maintaining, operating, and installing business equipment
* Business operation manual (e.g. McDonald's operation manual for franchisees)
* Supplier's information (contact person, product specifications, low-cost alternate suppliers).

Personnel Data

* Salaries and commissions of employees
* Members of a new project team
* Hiring, transfer or removal of key employees
* Evaluation of employee performance
* Employee's background
* Identification of the most talented employees
* Work force analysis
* Projected promotion data.

Financial Data

* Product costs
* Profit
* Pricing plans
* Manufacturer, supplier, dealer discounts
* Research and development budget
* Marketing and sales advertising budgets
* Methods for determination of cost/price for custom-built products or system
* Profit and loss statements
* Suppliers' prices.

13. PROPRIETARY INFORMATION IDENTIFICATION AND CLASSIFICATION

Documents and things must be classified in accordance with the established levels of secrecy. A rule of thumb for ascertaining the level of secrecy for sensitive information: "the benefit to competitors should be inversely proportional to the number of employees knowing such information." Department heads and managers must determine what data should be classified. Classified documents must be selected with discretion, in order not to ruin the credibility of the confidential information protection system.

Illustration of the information classification guidelines used by one corporation:

* top level (the most serious damage to the company if misappropriated): business and marketing strategies, technology and research data.
* middle level (significant harm to the business operations): customer list.

* initial level (records negatively affecting employees): medical, financial and other personnel-related records.[25]

Documents, samples, blueprints, manuals, and research or laboratory notebooks should have legends claiming proprietary rights, company's name, employee's name and be conspicuously marked "confidential" or "proprietary." That notice identifies proprietary information and warns the information user.

If trade secrets are not identified, at least in general terms, to the employees, then legal protection of such secrets may be lost. Therefore, company internal manuals, drawings, signs, confidentiality agreements, labels, intracompany meetings and memoranda should clarify what is considered to be a proprietary data. The most prevalent defense in business secret misappropriation cases is that there was no trade or business secret in the first place. Classification of information will help to prove in court the existence of business secrets.

Misappropriation of trade secrets may lead to recovery of actual and punitive damages, attorney's fees, injunctions (usually limited to the period needed to "reverse engineer" or independently develop the secret), and even criminal liability. A former employee who misappropriated the employer's trade secrets may be sued for unfair competition, conversion, unjust enrichment, economic espionage, breach of contract, tortious interference with contractual and business relations.

The ultimate penalty for infringing of proprietary property rights is an injunction, which in effect terminates any business activity with respect to the infringing product or process. A preliminary injunction is generally easier to obtain in trade secret cases than in patent litigation. Such an injunction forces many defendants to abandon their activities before a trial.

14. MEMORANDA

Written memoranda on classified information are to be avoided, if possible. Note of caution: Do not authorize putting in writing legal or technical opinions, unless the writer is qualified to do so. Memoranda to files, which must be kept secret, should be addressed to attorneys. Then memoranda cannot be produced at trial under the attorney-client privilege.

15. COPYRIGHTS

An original work of authorship, fixed in a tangible medium of expression for communication to other either directly or through a device, can be copyrighted, e.g., computer programs, pictures, maps, compilation of facts and so on. Computer programs may enjoy protection under the patent (in combination with a structure or a process), copyright and trade secret laws.

A copyright protects only the form of expression but not the underlying ideas, principles or facts, which therefore can be appropriated by anyone. For instance, facts contained in a copyrighted book can be used without any obligation to the author, but copying the book pages is improper. A copyright would protect the computer program itself but not the underlying techniques.

A copyright in a work created after January 1, 1978 lasts for the life of the author, or the last surviving co-author, plus fifty years, or 75 years for works by corporations. Works made "for hire" (usually belong to the employer, unless agreed otherwise in writing) are protected for the shorter of 100 years from the date of creation or 75 years from the date of first publication.

A copyright can be divided, and conveyed to different parties in increments, such as movie rights, publication rights, right to modify or use, and so on. A copyright can be sold, assigned or licensed (e.g., royalty paid per each performed show or sold copy).

It is a good idea to put a notice on all printed materials and "works of art," including manuals, advertisements, sales and promotional literature, and articles, promotional or training films, computer programs, and so on.

Copyright infringement may be punished by impounding all infringing copies, injunction, criminal actions against the infringer, awarding a copyright owner actual damages and profits (direct and indirect) of the infringer or statutory damages, attorney's fees and costs. Even advertising agency's profits may be awarded for infringement of copyright.[26]

Illustration of copyrightable items:

* Commercial advertisements (posters, illustrations, a picture, television commercial)[27]
* Manuals and parts catalogs (arrangement and manner of expression)
* Promotional literature, books
* Movies, choreographic performances and pictures
* Paintings, sculptures, toys, art and musical works
* Product labels, containers and packaging
* Greeting cards and posters
* Translated text

The Copyright Act (17 U.S.C.A. Sec.5) specifies classes of work which can be copyrighted.

16. KNOW-HOW

Know-how, which is technical and commercial information exceeding the bounds of common knowledge (i.e. having a certain originality), has an economic value. Know-how embraces the concept of trade secrets which require higher degree of novelty and originality. Know-how is usually associated with transfer of technology agreements. Such agreements may involve patents, trademarks and trade secrets. It is a good idea to allocate a separate royalty rate to each category in licenses that combine know-how and trade secrets with patents. If, for any reason, such patents are invalidated or become unenforceable, then the know-how or trade secret license (royalty) associated with these patents may remain intact in perpetuity.

Illustrations of "know-how" which could be sold or licensed:

(1) Delivery of models, blueprints, operational manuals and other documents.

(2) Construction of the facilities.

(3) Installation of equipment.

(4) Initial run of the equipment.

(5) Training of personnel.

(6) Ongoing technical assistance.

(7) Material and equipment specifications.

(8) Manufacturing data.

Know-how is gained through efforts, expenses and time, and that technical knowledge of developing products or systems for the employer belongs to this employer. Specific know-how may become a trade secret.[28]

Engineering know-how is the knowledge of putting together the system which may comprise of conventional components. That specific knowledge is distinguishable from the general knowledge and skill which belong to employees. The courts find it difficult to believe that ex-employees would not use their knowledge if they continue to work on the same products for a competitor.[29] Therefore, all trade secret protection methods discussed in this book have to be used in order to preserve the rights to and benefits arising from such type of proprietary information.

17. COURTS AND LAWSUITS

A lot of commercial secrets may be lost and uncovered during the litigation process. Unfair competition, patent and trade secret suits inherently involve disclosure of data and modus operandi of each party to these suits, and sometimes of other parties connected with such suits. Parties are not free to exempt data or limit the exposure of data. Parties may request the judge to: (a) exclude spectators and non-testifying witnesses from the court room ("gag order"); (b) request review of sensitive documents in the judge's chambers, when trade secret information is discussed at trial; (c) get a protective order embracing sensitive information ("attorney's eyes only"); and (d) seek exclusion of documents on the basis of attorney-client or another type of privilege. The judge has discretion to allow these requests. If the case is settled, the parties may keep the settlement agreement terms confidential.

18. INSURANCE

One of the losers in cases involving a theft of intellectual property (trade secrets, know-how) may be an insurance company which can be forced to pay the replacement cost of the stolen intangible assets. An insurance company may even absorb such a cost without being able to subrogate the loss from anyone, e.g. if an off-shore company, which purloined these secrets, goes bankrupt or changes its name, or is not amenable to the U.S. court jurisdiction. Therefore, each company must have an insurance coverage of such intangible assets.

For insurance purposes, business losses can be divided into two categories, direct and indirect. Direct losses include computer stored data, software, physical objects and products. Indirect losses comprise lost time due to interruption or work, expenses of replacement or repair of the systems, equipment and parts.

Security Liability Insurance for liability arising out of computer-generated, or otherwise created information, covers the disputes stemming from:

(a) negligence (errors due to lack of ordinary care to find them or train properly the personnel);

(b) disasters (fire, flood, power failures, ventilation outages, live and magnetic/radio frequency interference); and

(c) health protection of personnel.

There are numerous ways to safeguard proprietary information which were not examined in detail but should become a part of the protection program, such as training and educating the workforce, searching bags at the premises' exits, independent security audits and so on.

PART 5

SECURITY MEASURES
FOR CLASSIFIED DATA COURIERS

A carrier of important proprietary information heading to a meeting with competitors or suppliers may be an object of a planned robbery or kidnapping attack. One of the most valuable portable assets is a laptop computer containing secret information. Schemes for the theft of a laptop computer range from pickpocket techniques to a well planned action involving distraction by spilling a liquid on the target's suit or by asking questions, while other members of the team steal the computer. The stolen data may stiffen the opposition's negotiation terms or otherwise harm the party losing the data.

Key employees, information couriers and executives should be educated and trained in security steps needed for protecting them from kidnap attacks and the loss of valuable items. The following steps are the least expensive and most doable by the data couriers.

A. TRAVEL ARRANGEMENTS

The travel security plan starts from pre-travel arrangements. The following is a short list of prudent steps to be taken prior to the departure.

1. ENTRY DOCUMENTS

Make sure that your passport is valid, visas are current, accurate, properly designated as a business or tourist visa and appropriate for the designated country. Foreign customs and immigration authorities may detain travelers for a long period of time, and sometimes demand bribes, if there are errors in entry documents.

2. TRAVEL PLANS

You, your co-workers and family members should not disclose the travel itinerary to outsiders. A minimum number of people should be aware of your travel plans. Your itinerary can be obtained through telephone calls to secretaries, theft of your appointment book, calls to the travel agency, through acquaintances, electronic surveillance or otherwise. Flights, seat arrangements, transportation to and from stations and airports, car rentals, appointments, lodging arrangements must be confirmed. Have a travel companion or have a local representative meet you upon arrival at your destination. Have an emergency plan in case of any mishap en route to your destination.

3. CUSTOMS

Obtain a brochure describing the local customs rules from the consulates of the countries you intend to visit. The U.S. Customs Service helps the travelers with this kind of information. Violations of these rules may result in criminal (jail) and civil (financial) penalties, and the traveler may be branded (recorded in the customs' computer database) as an international smuggler. For more detailed discussion of the U.S. Customs rules, you may call the DENVICA 24-hour legal information bureau (1-900-680-6060) or request literature from the local U.S. Customs Service.

4. CURRENCY

Exchange currencies (at least enough to cover local transportation and meals) in your home country, thereby avoiding long lines, and surveillance by criminals, at foreign airport currency exchange booths.

5. TICKETS

Buy airplane tickets for non-stop flights. Select flights on large planes and do not sit in the aisle seats, since hijackers prefer planes with fewer passengers and the hostage taking or liberating activity mostly affects passengers seated in the aisle seats.

6. LUGGAGE

Do not place money, jewelry, cameras, glasses, prescribed medication or proprietary information documents in your checked luggage. In case of a hijacking, it is better to have these items in your pocket, briefcase, or a purse. Every luggage lock must have a different combination. Use hard wall luggage with strapping to prevent opening of the luggage in case of damage to the luggage locks. Do not leave the luggage unattended until it is taken away by the representatives of the common carrier (airline, shipping line, etc.). Do not take someone's packages for delivery to people at the destination and do not ask anyone to pack your luggage.

7. LUGGAGE TAGS

Use a name tag with a cover blocking the view of the name. No company name, company logo, home address, or business card must be attached to the luggage. Only your last name, business address and telephone number should be contained in the closed name tag. Put a card with your name and address inside every piece of luggage. The best to use is a Personal ID carrier produced by the Global Connection Corporation. See DENVICA-MALL at p. 145.

8. DOCUMENTS

Leave with a family member, a friend, or your office, one copy of carry-on sensitive documents, passport, visa, air tickets, travel and appointment schedules, credit cards, drivers license, international drivers permit, international innoculation record, prescription for glasses and medicine, medical card showing the blood type and special medical conditions, health and car insurance cards, and credit cards. The second copy should be put inside the checked luggage.

Keep in mind the fact that the sensitive documents could be copied by foreign authorities. Carry the minimum number of cards and documents. A Personal Data carrier combining majority of numbers and replacing scratches of paper is very useful for that purpose. These inexpensive and wallet-kept carriers can be purchased by calling the Global Connection Corporation toll-free number: 1-888-88-777-69.

9. INSURANCE

Get an insurance, or a company-sponsored fund, offering a bounty or reward for capturing the kidnappers. Kidnapping prices for a business executive may reach millions of dollars. For instance, Sanyo Corporation paid $2 million ransom for the release of Mamoru Konno, President of Sanyo Video Components Corp. USA, kidnapped on August 10, 1996, in Tijuana, Mexico.[1]

B. TRANSPORTATION

In general, the security rules are similar for all types of transportation used in foreign countries. However, certain distinctive steps are illustrated in the following comments.

1. AIRPORTS

Check in for the flight about three hours prior to the departure time since the lines for customs, immigration, security check points and ticket clearance can be very long. Do not take any items out of the packed luggage in public. Do not be a hero and avoid any commotion or disturbance. Avoid waiting in the areas open to the general public. Declare all money, checks or stocks you carry pursuant to law. Your luggage will be destroyed if left unattended. Do not rely on strangers sitting close to you at the airport or a train station to watch for your laptop computer and briefcase while you are going away for a few minutes.

2. TRAINS

Buy tickets at or through a hotel, local co-worker or a friend to avoid standing in lines at the railroad or bus terminals. Keep the train tickets until you leave the country. Check the train destination, change of train en route, train splitting and attachment to another train, track number and names of stations where the train stops before boarding the train. Buy a window seat for a quick escape if necessary. Keep all documents, tickets, passport and visa in the inside pocket at all times.

Keep the compartment door locked and request identification of those who want to entry the compartment. Know the train conductors by name and let them know if you must step out of the train. Avoid arriving late at night or early in the morning, unless a pick-up has been arranged in advance.

3. CARS

Have a good road guide and a map. Fasten the seat belt while driving a car. Carry your International Driving Permit and state drivers license. Buy the liability and collison insurance. Flash the lights while passing another car. The lane adjacent to the median strip is for the passing or high speed cars. Do not pick up or give a ride to unknown people. Inspect the rental car before entering it. Know how to use a stick shift transmission since most of the cars will probably have the manual transmission.

C. HOTELS

The following security tips associated with traveling to and from, registering and staying in a hotel can minimize the risks of being harmed.

(1) Watch your luggage until you surrender it to the bellman. Upon departure, keep the luggage claim checks together with the travel documents. You may need the proof of the storage of your luggage at the hotel. Luggage must touch your leg while you are awaiting someone. Lugggage kept in the room must be locked during your absence.

(2) Let the bellman carry your luggage to the room, check the rooms and give you instructions on use of the telephone, TV and heating equipment.

(3) Remember the hotel employees' uniforms, be suspicious of an uninvited visitor and request badge identification and front desk confirmation for a repairman visit.

(4) Do not leave any personal or classified documents, lap top computer, briefcases or cameras in a car or car glove compartment. If necessary, lock them up in a trunk. Carry a passport with you at all times.

(5) Park in lighted areas. If the car is surrendered to a valet service, leave only an ignition key in the car. All other keys must be removed from the car.

(6) Use your personal credit card, avoid naming your company in a hotel.

(7) Do not get out of the car if suspicious people are hanging around the parking area. Ask for an escort to the parked vehicle, if appropriate.

(8) Take a room key with you and do not leave it in the hotel's mail slot or box. A room key in the box is a sign of your absence from the hotel.

(9) Take mental notes of the distance from your room to the hotel stairways, public telephone locations, street names where the hotel is located, nearby bus, train or taxi stops. Get a city map from a concierge.

(10) Latch or chain the door and place a chair against the door when you go to bed.

(11) It is better to keep valuables in your local office. The hotel's safe deposit box is reviewed by foreign intelligence services. Double envelope the valuables, zigzag a line across the seam, tape the seams and edges prior to placing the valuables into the hotel safe deposit box. Room safes are good for keeping the valuables. Report the theft of any item to the front desk, insurance company and Consular Offices at the U.S. Embassy. Get a letter from the hotel acknowledging the incident.

(12) Consult with the concierge about the taxi cab charges, indicia and reputation, and ask about safe areas for jogging and dining.

(13) Sign your room number for any purchase in the hotel instead of giving cash.

(14) Do not invite strangers to your room, to avoid theft or criminal attack.

(15) Get a room not higher than the seventh floor since a local fire deparment may not have a ladder to reach a higher floor.

(16) In case of fire, take a room key when leaving the room, do not use elevators, cover your nose and mouth with a wet towel or shirt, open the window, soak blankets and towels in the tub and place them onto the vents and cracks around the doors so to seal them and stay close to the floor.

(17) Beware of unauthorized taxi cabs having no appropriate cab indicia. Agree on the price prior to entering the cab. Have the destination address written on a piece of paper to avoid confusion and misunderstanding.

D. BUSINESS AND SOCIAL CONDUCT

Business negotiations or delivery of important proprietary information can be compromised due to the traveler's misconduct or activity. Such inappropriate activity or surveillance by criminals or intellligence services are examined in the following sections.

(1) Realize that every comment or statement about the company's business plans, customers, product ingredients, any research, personal traits of company employees, your own or co-worker's financial or marital problems will be used by the company competitors. Do not say or do anything which would cause the company's loss of face or delay in consummating the deal.

(2) Do not get entangled with illegal currency exchange or illegal drug purchase, use, transportation, or sale. Drink very moderately to avoid loss of mental capacity and control over your senses at social gatherings regardless of local guest requests and admonitions. Carry doctor's prescription for the medications containing narcotic substance. Get legal permission to export any painting or antique item out of the country.

(**3**) Beware of any stranger trying to develop a relationship by appearing at the social functions where you are present, initiating a conversation about your work, politics, foreign language. Talkative strangers eager to engage you in small talk, offer a ride or invite you to dinner can be intelligence operatives.

Stay away from romantic involvements.

(**4**) Presume that you are followed by the opposition, your telephones the hotel room are bugged, and documents left in the hotel's safe deposit box or in the room are copied. Do what you should do, say what you have to say but remember that everything is being recorded for blackmail or intelligence collection. Use a communication code discussed previously in this book for discussing the negotiation in progress or conveying the sensitive information to colleagues. Write notes instead of talking or naming the paries, amounts or contract terms. Upon noticing the surveillance activity, consult with the consulate and follow their advice.

E. HIJACKING AND KIDNAPPING

There are basic rules for targets of kidnapping or victims of the hijacking. The U.S. State Department publications, such as *Emergency Planning Guidelines for American Businesses Abroad, Security Guidelines for American Families Living Abroad, Guidelines for Protecting U.S. Business Information Overseas, Personal Security Guidelines for the American Traveler Overseas,* are available through the Overseas Security Advisory Council or U. S. Government Printing Office. The following is a brief list of pertinent instructions based on the American government recommendations.

1. CONDUCT DURING HIJACKING

In order to survive the hijacking ordeal, comply with the hijackers instructions. Concentrate on memorizing the hijackers voice, accent, facial features, dress, hands, gait, scars, behavior. Upon request, surrender the passport and personal belongings. If you or someone else needs to go to a restroom or requires medical assistance, ask a vehicle crew member first. Answer questions in very short sentences without volunteering any information.

If there is a chance to escape, take it only if you are mentally ready to kill or be killed. Hesitation in executing any escape maneuver can be lethal. Do not make the hijackers angry or become suspicious of you. In order not to become a casualty of a rescue operation, follow the rescue team instructions very quickly. If you hear gunfire, noise, screaming outside or inside the vehicle, keep your head down, drop to the floor, or squat in the corner. Cooperate with investigators of the hijacking operation.

2. KIDNAPPING

There is no best time to escape the kidnapping process. It depends on who, where and how executes the operation.

(1) If the kidnapping takes place in a public place or a hotel room, make noise, drop furniture items, bump into hotel employees, trip and fall down, hit the wall or otherwise bring attention to you for registering the time and place of the occurrence.

(2) If possible, press a preprogrammed emergency button on your cellular telephone or "record" buttons on your tape recorder.

(3) If you have been blindfolded or locked in a car trunk, concentrate on memorizing the noise, smell, turns, change of car directions, and the time spans between the above points registered in your memory.

(4) Give the interrogators publicly available information. Do not make admissions against your own interest. Give short answers. "I cannot recall this at the moment" is an acceptable answer. Stay calm. Fix your eyesight on any spot on the wall or a desk. Stick to your story. Do not sign any papers, unless physically forced to. Fake illness and fatigue. Do not argue with the captors.

(5) If detained for a long time, exercise mentally and physically, memorize the captors voice, gait, habits, names, nicknames, facial features, schedule, family attachments. Keep track of days, dates, places, layouts of rooms and buildings, smell, noise, sounds. Always think about the escape possibilities. If you escape, get to an embassy of your country first or a friendly government.

In case of emergency, American citizens can seek help from the U.S. Department of State (visas, innoculation, passports) by calling 1-202-647-5225; or the Overseas Security Advisory Council at 1-202-663-0533; or the International Trade Administration, U.S. Department of Commerce at 1-800-USA-TRADE or 1-800-872-8723.

F. SELF-DEFENSE

Do not attempt to use any martial arts technique, unless you have been trained to do so for years. You will have one chance to attack. Do it right or not at all. There may be no other chance for you. The unpublicized self-defense strategies are:

(1) Stand in such a way that the light source (sun, suspended lights, etc.) are located behind you and facing your attacker.

(2) Blind the attacker with tobacco from a squeezed cigarette, sand, dust, ash, a poke into the eye by a finger, pen, key, fork, umbrella or any other available object in order to deliver an incapacitating strike.

(3) Do not try to release the attacker's grabs. A grab or a grip is a favor to you since the holding hand becomes immobilized and renders the attacker defense-free. Upon grabbing, kick the attacker's shins, knees, groin, or clap the ears with palms, or strike the throat, eyes or nose. Quickly repeat the strikes, if necessary.

(4) Kicks shall not be higher than a knee level. Punches can be effective if you have been trained to punch for a long time. Otherwise, you can hurt yourself and cause no significant harm to the assailant. The simplest hand strikes are the hammer fist strikes where the point of impact is the bottom of the fist. These strikes can be deadly if applied against the vital organs, such as the back of the head, heart, kidney or rib cage. Elbow strikes can be effective in close quarter combat situations, where the assailant is behind, aside or directly in front of you.

(5) Avoid situations where you can be cornered. Use the environment for self-defense, for example, striking the assailant's face with a water glass while holding its bottom in your palm.

(6) Stunning techniques: palm or fist to the nose or lips, kicks to shins, achilles tendons (attacking from behind), knee or groin, stomps on attacker's feet, elbow to the jaw or temple, or clapping the ears with both palms. These techniques cause temporary pain and immobilize the opponent for the short time needed either to escape or complete the self-defense with more damaging strikes.

(7) The majority of weapon-free killing techniques are based on strikes to the windpipe, temple, back of the head, back of the neck, strangulation, twisting the head or snapping the head backward. These techniques must be used in extreme situations where your or your family member's life is in danger.

(8) Do not wrestle with or take weapons away from the attacker. First, deflect the hand with a weapon with a palm or step aside the weapon, to be outside the line of fire or the weapon trajectory. Second, immediately push the attacker's head against the wall or other hard object, or shove the attacker into the path of a moving vehicle, or use the above mentioned stunning and killing techniques.

(9) Ask a question and strike the assailant while he is talking. The idea is that a person cannot strike with power while talking. Take weapons away only when the attacker is incapacitated and direct (deflect) the weapons away from your body while "stripping" the attacker from these weapons.

(10) Distract the assailant's attention with statements, such as "Here is a police officer," pointing a finger or raising the hand toward the skies or a certain object, turning away or dropping a wallet or a glass to the ground, immediately prior to your strike.

(11) If surrounded by multiple assailants, negotiate your way out and, if that is impossible, attack first. Use the keys or a pen to strike the hollow of the throat, ear opening or eye; bite the nose, windpipe, ear or lip off; or bite the skin off on the wrist or hollow of the elbow. Assailant's bleeding and your determination to fight may cause the crowd to hesitate, thereby giving you time for escape.

(12) Do not fear pain or injury. Fear is not an objective thing. Fear exists only in your head. To concentrate on the attack and diminish the fear, exhaust air forcefully, hold your your breath, slowly inhale. Strike while holding your breath or exhaling.

If you decide to attack, do so with everything you have got. Speed is more important than mass since any increase in speed doubles the energy of impact. Screaming is good for scaring the opponent and adding power to the strike. But one should know when and how to scream. In general, silent strikes are more effective.

You will succeed with the escape or self-defense, if your mental state, not your muscles, allows you to do so.

G. GUARDING PROPRIETARY INFORMATION

Like anything else in life, use common sense and be alert. Information in your possession, or accessible to you, is valuable for competitors and criminals. That is why you may become a target of an attack or recruitment by private or government agencies. Think about your mission and your family. The security measures described below can be adopted not only for travelling overseas but for the daily modus operandi.

(1) Change frequently your home-work or hotel-work routes, and arrival and departure times. Try to be alert (no dozing off) while keeping sensitive material with you and stay in the crowded places. Be cognizant of the eavesdropping on your cellular telephone conversations, laptop computer text, documents disclosing travel or marketing plans, or other business secrets, which may be audio and video recorded by the airplane seat "neighbors" or hotel employees.

(2) Preprogram emergency numbers on your cellular telephone for one key (touch) dialing, including embassy, police, ambulance, local representative and your office numbers. Do not keep secret data on the computer hard disk but rather on the diskette carried on you at all times. Encrypt the data contained on the diskette with off-the-shelf software using Triple DES encryption code or elliptic curve encryption algorithms.

(3) Do not leave the sensitive documents in a hotel room, or hotel's safe deposit box, as they may be photographed or copied. Do not show off in any manner, such as traveling in expensive cars and wearing glitzy clothing and jewelry.

(4) Handcuff a hand (by a lockable plastic strip) to an attache case or a computer case with valuable items. Carry a pocket camera or pocket taperecorder for recording of vehicle license plate numbers, objects and people involved in assaults or emergency situations.

(5) Avoid standing close to the edge of a subway platform or a street sidewalk curb and beware of situations where you may be pushed into the path of a moving vehicle.

(6) Motorcycle riders rob and snatch purses from people walking down the street. Avoid walking close to the curb. Carry a purse with a strap over your shoulder and on the hip adjacent to your companion or away from the road curb.

There are numerous other security measures, such as employing bodyguards, driving in armored cars, wearing bulletproof vests, learning defensive driving, etc. However, discrete appearance and adherence to the above rules may be as effective as more expensive and exotic defensive techniques.

PART 6

ENFORCEMENT OF PROPRIETARY RIGHTS IN THE U.S.A.

Enforcement of the laws against the proprietary information or intellectual property pirates on a worldwide scale means bringing to justice any individual or company in the United States and other countries. There are numerous state and federal laws which can be used to protect trade secrets and other types of intangible assets.

Illustrations of new international laws which can be invoked under some circumstances:

1. THE ECONOMIC ESPIONAGE ACT OF 1996

Under the U.S. Economic Espionage Act of 1996, foreign organizations and governments may be penalized for stealing, or benefitting from theft, of U.S. companies' trade secrets by payment of fines up to $10,000,000 and for convicted individuals up to $500,000. American-on-American trade secret theft (including receiving, buying or possessing of misappropriated property) is punishable by fines up to $5,000,000 for organizations and fines plus imprisonment up to 10 years for individuals. In addition, the Act provides for criminal forfeiture to the United States of any property and proceeds derived from such theft.

This Act may be used by foreign companies and governments against the U.S. companies and individuals (citizen or permanent resident alien) for conduct occurring outside the United States or an act in furtherance of the offense which was committed in the United States.[1]

2. COPYRIGHT PROTECTION UNDER THE GATT ACCORD OF 1994

Under the Uruguay Rounds Agreements Act of the General Agreement on Tariffs and Trade (GATT) of 1994, as of January 1, 1996, U.S. copyright owners received wider protection abroad. But the GATT accord now affords protection to foreign copyright owners (144 countries) and allows them to seek compensation from U.S. organizations for the use of coyrighted works which were in the public domain heretofore. Based on that new law, foreign owners requested stopping the use of images of French artists on scarves sold by the Metropolitan Museum of Modern Arts in New York; the mare and foal images on 3.5 million Kentucky vehicle license plates, and on the Kentucky Horse Park logo, allegedly derived from a German photographer's picture; etc.[2]

In addition to international laws, there are national laws which could be applied to misappropriation of proprietary information and trade secrets.

3. THE RACKETEER INFLUENCED AND CORRUPT ORGANIZATION ACT (RICO)

The Act (18 U.S.C. Sec. 1962) can be used to punish the counterfeiting of copyrighted goods and misappropriation of trade secrets. Using mail or wire to steal trade secrets (mail or wire fraud), or receiving payment for counterfeit or stolen goods by wrongdoers would violate the statute. The statute prohibits selling and distribution, or offering for unlawful use any "counterfeit article", such as protected by a copyright or trademark. A successful civil RICO action results in the mandatory award or treble damages, attorney's fees, equitable relief (injunctions, i.e. stopping wrongful activity) and costs.

4. THE NATIONAL STOLEN PROPERTY ACT (18 U.S.C. SEC. 2314)

Transportation in interstate or foreign commerce of any goods, wares, or merchandise of the value of $5,000 or more with the knowledge that the same have been stolen, converted, or taken by fraud violates the statute. Value includes tangible components and information which must be embodied in a tangible carrier, such as computer hardware or software embodied in discs. Under the National Stolen Property Act, the wrongdoer may be both fined not more than $10,000 and imprisoned for not more the 10 years.

Illustration:

Hitachi was convicted under this Act for industrial espionage (paying more than $500,000 to FBI agents posing as electronics black marketers for stealing IBM trade secrets and using them in their computers); settled a civil suit with IBM (by paying the legal cost) for illegally using IBM software in the past; and entered into eight-year software license agreement (paying about a billion yen a month).[3]

5. THE ELECTRONIC COMMUNICATIONS PRIVACY ACT OF 1986

The Act provides for the civil injunction of illegal interception of oral communications; fine or imprisonment for not more than a year, or both, for intentionally accessing without authorization a facility and obtaining, altering or preventing authorized access to electronically stored communications; one year in jail and fine, or both, for installing a trap and track device on wire or electronic communication. The Act prohibits unauthorized access to and interception of e-mail communications and e-mail storage in a computer system.

Other federal criminal statutes, such as Travel Act (18 U.S.C.A. Sec. 1952); Mail Fraud (18 U.S.C.A. Sec. 1341; Wire Fraud (18 U.S.C.A. Sec. 1343); and Counterfeit Access Device and Computer Fraud and Abuse Act of 1984 (18 U.S.C.A. Sec. 1030) may be invoked to prosecute some of the trade secret misappropriation cases.

Besides traditional enforcement of proprietary rights under state trade secret and unfair competition laws, as well as federal patent and copyright laws, other methods are often invoked in order to seek justice in the United States. These routes by-pass traditional court based litigation between an aggrieved party and individual transgressors.

Here are some of these nontraditional legal avenues:

6. INTERNATIONAL TRADE COMMISSION (ITC)

Many ITC cases involve the importation into the United States of "knock off" products which infringe: a U.S. patent covering a product or the process used to make such products; a common law or registered trademark; or a registered copyright. The ITC can issue cease and desist orders or exclude violating articles from entry into the United States in order to prevent injury to a respective domestic industry.

If there are numerous importers of the alleged infringing products, a multiplicity of lawsuits would usually be necessary to stop the infringing importers. The ITC action stops the imported articles, although not the importer, thereby providing practical relief within a relatively short period of time (about one year).

In one case of misappropriated trade secrets involving the manufacturing of skinless sausage casings, the U.S. Court of Appeals for the Federal Circuit affirmed the ITC's 10-year exclusion order against a Spanish firm (Viscofan, S.A.) for violation of Sec. 337 of the Tariff Act of 1980. "The duration of relief in a case of misappropriation of trade secrets should be the period of time it would have taken respondent independently to develop the technology using lawful means," i.e. time to create the whole manufacturing process and not the time needed to discover each trade secret independently.[4]

7. U.S. CUSTOMS SERVICE

The U.S. Customs Service was established in 1789 to collect the revenue for the United States by taxing imports. The Customs Service has many other missions, such as seizing the products infringing on the intellectual property rights (copyright, trademark, patent) of U.S. owners thereof, preventing piracy of the recorded (video and audio) works of art and entry of substandard goods and illegal drugs. The Customs Service protects 96,000 miles of sea and land borders from the entry of contraband and smugglers.

More than 450 million travelers pass annually through Customs. Thousands of tons of numerous goods come through the borders daily. Because it is physically impossible to examine each container, the inspectors selectively target cargo for clearance. Usually, imports from high risk countries and manufacturers of products which violated the U.S. laws in the past are the primary targets for such inspection. About one half of one percent of merchandise is randomly selected for thorough inspection.

Foreign-made products infringing on U.S. copyrights and trademarks can be confiscated by the U.S. Customs Service at all points of entry of such products into the United States. Forfeited articles can be destroyed or returned to the country of export at the owner's expense. Copyright and trademark registration with the U.S. Customs Service is a prerequisite for seizure and forfeiture of infringing articles. Only trademarks and copyrights registered in the United States Patent and Trademark Office can be registered with the Customs Service.

Illustration of the Customs Service assistance in copyright infringement protection:

The U.S. Customs Service in Seattle determined (compared the copyrighted IBM software with the infringing software) that software used in FX-800 computers manufactured by Matsushita Electric Industrial Co. Ltd. was similar to the IBM software. The manufacturer admitted copyright infringement, stopped exports of these computers to the United States, and paid a fine to IBM.[5]

In summary, the U.S. Customs Service is a private industry ally which for a small fee will protect the U.S. patent, trademark and copyright owners from pirating their products and services by foreign companies.

PART 7

IMPLEMENTATION OF INFORMATION THEFT COUNTERMEASURES

The industrial security and legal protection steps discussed above represent only a minor fraction of the system covering technical and nontechnical aspects of corporate intelligence collection and protection. Such system is pieced together with the help of security experts, attorneys, computer security consultants and representatives of each department. There are more than one hundred procedures which must be put together and maintained for the successful business operation. These procedures range from education, building loyalty and training of the personnel to information flow control and securing rights to the existing intangible assets.

Commercial espionage penetrates every industry and it will thrive as long as there is competition. Nothing will stop intelligence gathering activity and loss of proprietary information. Implementation of a comprehensive business protection system integrating industrial security measures with legal protection measures will benefit any business by raising its profitability through utilization and preservation of the existing resources. Such a system may help to minimize "brain raids", reduce losses of sales and services to competition, avoid needless lawsuits, recover R & D expenses, increase negotiating power, add assets and tax benefits, and generate extra income.

The investment of money and efforts into industrial intelligence countermeasures is minuscule in comparison with the benefits derived from the implemented and maintained security system. Such investment must be compared with the financial consequences resulting from the losses of business, name, reputation, jobs and business investments. The U.S. government is spending billions of dollars on protection of secret documents, let alone other security-related expenses.

Illustration:

The Director of the Information Security Oversight Office reported to the U.S. Congress that the U.S. government fiscal 1996 cost of keeping secret documents is $2,741,987,125. This $2.7 billion does not include cost of keeping secret records by private companies working on government contracts. Cost to pay and operate the entire U.S. Congress will be approximately equal to that amount.[1]

Identification, utilization and protection of trade secrets, business know-how and other proprietary information is as important as marketing, research, manufacturing, accounting and sales. It is perhaps even more important because the whole business venture may be lost due to misappropriation of proprietary information.

PART 8

SEMINARS

To determine how to assemble, implement and maintain such a system, as well as identify and capitalize on your own business know-how and trade secrets, you may arrange a one-day on site seminar "Commercial Espionage: Protection and Exploitation of Proprietary Business Information." The seminars are organized by the Global Connection Corporation of Skokie, Illinois, U.S.A. E-mail address: global @ denvica-mall.com.

Valuable proprietary information means any information the loss of which to competitors would be detrimental to its owner, namely, marketing and business plans, customer and supplier identities, product and economic research, work force analysis, modus operandi, new product introduction and price discount plans, and so forth.

Business information is an intangible asset which may be sold, exchanged, licensed, depreciated and misappropriated. It may be lost or acquired through employees, customers, negotiation, sales literature, and numerous economic espionage methods. Loss of such trade secrets to competitors may result in the diminished sales and customer base, and could lead to the business demise.

This seminar will benefit your business by showing how to:

* Properly release data to the public and private parties;
* Protect documents, facilities, computer data and products;
* Identify and secure rights to trade secrets and know-how;
* Generate revenue off and exploit the hidden assets;
* Avoid needless and business damaging lawsuits;
* Implement a comprehensive information protection system;
* Minimize "brain raids" and loss of data through employees;
* Negotiate business deals;
* Find information leak sources;
* Legally acquire competitors' secrets;
* Enforce your own proprietary rights;
* Counter industrial espionage efforts.

Executives, marketing, sales and security personnel, attorneys, designers and computer system managers need to know these corporate information protection and exploitation measures.

CONCLUSION

The most confidential commercial secrets can be learned by determined competitors. Economic espionage is an inalienable part of competition. Technical sleuthing is proliferating with the speed of scientific progress. This book described the commercial war techniques which have been used and will be used throughout the world. Always. Anywhere. This book provides knowledge which may be used both as a sword and as a shield. Forewarned is forearmed.

Engineers and scientists may lose their belabored technical innovations. Financial institutions and service industries may lose their research, client data and public trust as result of the improper activity disclosure. Thousands of jobs could be terminated. Illustrations given in the book showed that.

Any business may collapse as a result of misappropriation of trade secrets and know-how. Years of blood, sweat, and tears spent for building a business enterprise, creating a new formula, device, method, or program will be for naught. Only the debts, ruined health, taxes, and unpleasant memories will stay with victims of economic espionage.

Intelligence-gathering activity may not be completely stopped but the risk of losing proprietary business information and valuable intangible assets may be significantly minimized. Preventive steps act like roadblocks to continuously moving industrial espionage vehicles. The more barriers, the better chance of success in countering the onslaught. This book examined various counterespionage, as well as physical and legal protection measures.

The seminars mentioned above will amplify and expand the knowledge of modern equipment, methods and laws used in combatting loss of intellectual property. Learning such information will help to gain competitive advantage, generate extra revenue and prevent a business demise. You should know how to protect your know how.

Good luck in all your endeavors.

REFERENCES

PART 1

INTANGIBLE COMMODITY:
PROPRIETARY INFORMATION/BUSINESS SECRETS

1. Ronald E. Yates, "Espionage Fight Shifts to Corporate Battlefield", *Chicago Tribune,* Business, p. 1, March 24, 1996.
2. "GE, as Victim, Testifies to Cost of Spying," *Chicago Tribune,* November 16, 1986.
3. "Industrial Espionage Sends You to Jail," *Economist,* January 12, 1980, p. 72.
4. Ronald E. Yates, "Free Enterprise Faces a New Threat from Abroad: Spies," *Chicago Tribune,* December 27, 1994, (Bus. Section), p. 4.
5. Gary Borg, "Japan Calls for Explanation of Reported CIA Eavesdropping," *Chicago Tribune,* Sec.1, October 17, 1995.
6. "Paper: CIA Spying on Trade Rivals," *Chicago Tribune,* Sec. 1, July 24, 1995.
7. Ronald E. Yates, *"Foreign Intelligence Agencies Have New Targets-U.S. Companies," Chicago Tribune*, Sec. 7, August 29, 1993.
8. Daniel Greenberg, "High-tech America's myopic mind-set," *U.S. News and World Report,* September 22, 1986.
9. Richard J. Heffernan and Dan T. Swartwood, *Trends in Intellectual Property Loss, Special Report*, The 1995 ASIS Survey, presented at the ASIS Annual Seminar on September 12, 1995 in New Orleans, U.S.A.

PART 2

CORPORATE INTELLIGENCE COLLECTION TECHNIQUES

1. *Baxley v. Black*, 224 Ga. 456, 162 S.E. 2d 389 (1968).
2. *Smokenders v. Smoke No More, Inc.*, 184 U.S.P.Q. 309 (S.D. Fla. 1974)
3. *Financial Programs, Inc. v. Falcon Financial Services, Inc.*, 371 F.Supp. 770 (D.Or. 1974).
4. *A.H. Emery Co. v. Marcan Products Corp.*, 389 F.2d 11 (2d Cir. 1968), cert. denied, 393 U.S. 835 (1968).
5. *Herrlein v. Kanakis*, 526 F.2d 252, 253 (7th Cir. 1975).
6. *Telex Corp. v. IBM*, 367 F. Supp. 258, 315-323, 357-359 (N.C. Okla. 1973), affirmed in part and rev'd in part, 510 F.2d 894 (10th Cir., 1975), cert. den., 423 U.S. 802, 96 S.Ct. 8 (1975).
7. "Brokerage Fined for Employee Raid," *Chicago Tribune,* Saturday, May 4, 1996, Business, p. 1.
8. Ann Hughey, "We Are a Soft Target," *Forbes,* September 15, 1980, p. 42.
9. Ronald E. Yates, "Foreign Intelligence Agencies Have New Targets-U.S. Companies," *Chicago Tribune,* August 29, 1993, Section 7, p. 6.
10. *U.S. News & World Report,* May 25, 1981.
11. Id. note 19.
12. Gillard and Smith, "Computer Crime: A Growing Threat," *Byte,* October, 1983, p. 398.
13. Id. note 21.
14. Id. note 21.
15. Richard Eels and Peter Nehemkis, *"Corporate Intelligence and Espionage",* 1984, McMillan Publishing Co., New York.
16. David Buchan, *"Old Hands Uncover New Tricks: Soviet Industrial Espionage,"* Financial Times, August 31, 1983 p. 11.
17. John Greenwald, "Corporate Cloak and Dagger: New Efforts are

Under Way to Stop an Epidemic of Industrial Espionage," *Time,* August 30, 1982 p. 62.

18. Richard Eels, Peter Nehemkis, *"Corporate Intelligence and Espionage,"* 1984.

19. Watson, Clark and Marro, "No Place to Hide," *Newsweek,* September 8, 1975.

20. Watson, Clark and Marro, "No Place to Hide," *Newsweek,* September 8, 1975.

21. *The Washington Post,* December 4, 1983.

22. "British Security Industry Grows," *Chicago Tribune,* February 16, 1988.

23. The *"Electronic Communications Piracy Act of 1986,"* 18 U.S.C.A. Sec. 2701 et seq., 1986.

24. Gary Borg, "Japan Calls for Explanation of Reported CIA Eavesdropping," *Chicago Tribune,* October 17, 1995, Sec. 1, p. 4.

25. *U.S. News & World Report,* June 26, 1978.

26. "Executive Gets Two-year Sentence for Industrial Espionage," *The Associated Press,* October 6, 1981 (Business News Section).

27. "The Publicity Effect of IBM Sting," *The New York Times,* November 5, 1983, (Late City Final Edition) at 37.

28. Ann Hughey, "We Are a Soft Target', *Forbes,* September 15, 1980, at 42.

29. Ronald E. Yates, "Espionage Fight Shifts to Corporate Battlefield," *Chicago Tribune,* Business, at 1, March 24, 1996.

30. Kathy Bergen, "As Technology Makes Advances So Does the Sophistication of Corporate Espionage," *Chicago Tribune,* Business, at 1, 1997.

31. *E.I. DuPont de Nemours & Co. v. Christopher,* 431 F.2d 1012, 166 U.S.P.Q. 421 (1970), cert. denied, 400 U.S. 1024, rehearing denied, 401 U.S. 967 (1971).

32. "Public Gets a Rare Sniff of Skunk Works Project," *Chicago Tribune,* August 10, Section 2, 1996.

33. Michael Saunders, *Protecting Your Business Secrets,* 1985.

34. *U.S. News & World Report,* May 25, 1981.

35. Id. note 43.

36. *Business Week,* September 20, 1982.

37. "Report: U.S. Firm Sold Nuclear Gear to Soviets," *Chicago Tribune,* November 9, 1995.

38. *Chicago Tribune,* June 4 and December 18, 1986.

39. *Chicago Tribune,* Thursday, June 12, Sec. A, 1986.

40. "German Spilled Missile Secrets, Paper Says," *Chicago Tribune,* December 13, Sec. 1, 1986.

41. Bill Richards, "Secret Stealth Fighter Is a Best-Seller (In 12-Inch Plastic-Assembly Required)," *The Wall Street Journal,* August 20, 1986.

42. Sanchez DeGramont "The Secret War" cited by Eels and Nehemkis in "Corporate Intelligence & Espionage", supra.

43. *Official Airlines Schedule Information Service, Inc. (OASIS) v. Eastern Air Lines, Inc.,* 333 F.2d 672, 141 U.S.P.Q. (5th Cir. 1964).

44. *U.S. News & World Report,* October 27, 1986.

45. "Official News Leaks Common, Study Finds," *Chicago Tribune,* December, 1986.

46. *Reginald Dale, "U.S. Conservatives on the Offensive in Right-to-know Battle," American News Sec., Financial Times,* April 2, 1985, Sec. 1, at 6.

47. Penton/IPC, *Industry Week,* May 27, 1985.

48. Peter J. Howe, "Engineering Student Causes A Flap With Novel Nautical Motor," *Chicago Tribune,* May 25, 1997, Sec. 12.

49. "Imitators are Hot on Designer Scents," *USA Today,* May 19, 1986.

50. Ed Magnuson, "Some of Our Chips are Missing: Trying to Keep U.S. High-Tech Exports from Moscow," *Time,* March 14, 1983.

51. *Cadillac Gage Co. v. Verne Engineering Corp.,* 203 U.S.P.Q. (BNA) 473 (Mich. Cir. Ct. 1978).

52. Glickman, *"Franchising,"* Matthew Bender, 1982.

53. *U.S. News & World Report,* May 25, 1981.

54. *Drill Parts & Service Co., Inc. v. Joy Mfg. Co.,* 223 U.S.P.Q. 521 (Ala. 1983).
55. Robert Johnson, "Inside Job: The Case of Marc Faith Shows Corporate Spies Aren't Just High Tech," *The Wall Street Journal,* at 1, January 9, 1987.
56. Ronald E. Yates, "Security Scandal Entangles Japanese Firms," *Chicago Tribune,* June 15, 1987, Sec. 4.
57. Id. note 64.
58. "British Security Industry Grows," *Chicago Tribune,* February 16, 1988.

PART 3

LOSSES OF PROPRIETARY DATA

1. Ronald E. Yates, "Espionage Fight shifts to Corporate Battlefield," *Chicago Tribune,* March 24, 1996, Business, p. 1.
2. Id. note 2.
3. Penton/IPC, *Industry Week,* May 27, 1985.

PART 4

SAFEGUARDING PROPRIETARY INFORMATION

A. RISK MANAGEMENT AND STRATEGIC PLANNING

1. Ronald E. Yates, "Foreign Intelligence Services Have New Targets- U.S. Companies," *Chicago Tribune,* August 29, 1993, (Bus. Sect.), p. 6.

B. INDUSTRIAL SECURITY

2. Moscal, "Sharing Family Secrets," *Industry Week,* February 17, 1986, p. 51.

3. Bob Wiedrich, "Spies, Mob Use Paper to Wash Away Worries," *Chicago Tribune*, December 28, 1986, Sec. 1.

4. *KFC Corp. v. Marion-Kay Co., Inc.*, 620 F. Supp. 1161 (S.D. Ind. 1985).

5. *Chicago Tribune*, Sec. 1, August 12, 1986.

6. *Johns-Mansville Corp. V. Guardian Industries Corp.*, 221 U.S.P.Q. 319 (E.D. Mich. 1983).

7. Maurice Paisley, "Police Crack Secret El Rukn Crime Code", *Chicago Tribune*, December 14, 1986.

8. *"Ever See a Flying Manatee?,"* *Chicago Tribune*, April 6, 1997, Sec. 12, p. 7.

C. LEGAL PROTECTION OF INTELLECTUAL PROPERTY

9. *Sperry Rand Corp. v. Pentronix, Inc.*, 311 F. Supp. 910 (E.D. Pa 1970).

10. *Digital Development Corp. v. International Memory Systems*, 185 U.S.P.Q. 136 (S.D. Cal. 1973).

11. *Data General Corp. v. Digital Computer Controls, Inc.*, 357 A.2d 105 (Del. Cir. 1975).

12. *Structural Dynamics Research Corp. v. Engineering Mechanics Research Corp.*, 401 F.Supp. 1102, 1114-15 (E.D. Mich. 1975).

13. *Electronic Data Systems v. Powell*, 524 S.W. 2d 393 (1975).

14. *Harrison v. Glucose Sugar Ref. Co.*, 116 F. 304 (7th Cir. 1902).

15. *The New York Times*, April 1, 1984 (Late City Final Edition), p.1.

16. *Wilson v. Barton & Ludwig, Inc.*, 220 U.S.P.Q. 375 (Ga. Ct. of App. 1982), (business management method).

17. *Moss, Adams & Co. v. Shilling*, 179 Cal. App. 3d 124 (Cal. App. 1 Dist. 1986).

18. *Smith International, Inc. v. Hughes Tool Co.*, 664 F.d 1373, 215 U.S.P.Q. 592 (9th Cir., Jan. 7, 1982).

19. "Kodak patent fight loses in top court," *Chicago Tribune*, October 7, 1986; *Polaroid Corp. v. Eastman Kodak Co.*, 228

U.S.P.Q. 305 (D. Mass. 1985).

20. *Alderman v. Tandy Corp.*, 222 U.S.P.Q. 806 (11th Cir., Fla.1983).

21. Maurice Paisley, "Chicken Chain Cries Afoul," *Chicago Tribune,* November 2, 1986, Sec. 3.

22. *Wilson Certified Food, Inc. v. Fairbury Food Products, Inc.,* 370 F. Supp. 108 (D. Neb. 1974), (bacon bits manufacturing process was known in the industry and, thus, did not get trade secret protection).

23. *Com-Share, Inc. v. Computer Complex, Inc.,* 338 F. Supp. 1229 (E.D.Mich. 1971), aff'd, 458 F.2d 1341 (6th Cir. 1972).

24. *Defiance Button Machine Co. v. C & C Metal Products Corp.,* 225 U.S. P.Q. 797 (2nd Cir. N.Y., 1985).

25. James A. Schweitzer, "Why Classify," *Security Management,* February 1989.

26. *Sid & Mary Kraft Television v. McDonald's Corp.,* 221 U.S.P.Q. 114, 117 (D.C. Cal. 1983).

27. *Bleistein v. Donaldson Lithographing Co.,* 23 S.Ct. 298 (1903).

28. *SI Handling Systems, Inc. v. Heisley,* 222 U.S.P.Q 53 (E. D. Penn. 1984).

29. Id. note 20.

PART 5

SECURITY MEASURES FOR CLASSIFIED DATA COURIERS

1. *Sun-Times,* Nation, "Kidnapped Japanese Exec Celebrates Family Reunion," August 21, 1996.

PART 6

ENFORCEMENT OF PROPRIETARY RIGHTS in the U.S.A.

1. 18 U.S.C. Ch. 90, Sec. 1831, et seq.
2. Wes Smith, "U.S. Finds Tables Turned On Copyright Protection," *Chicago Tribune*, March 17, 1997.
3. *The Nihon Keizai Shimbun, Japan Economic Journal,* December 6, 1983.
4. *Viscofan, S.A. v. U.S. International Trade Commission,* (CAFC, 1986), BNA, Vol. 31, at 434.
5. "Matsushita Admits FX-800 Infringed on IBM Software," *Chicago Tribune*, February 25, 1987.

PART 7

IMPLEMENTATION OF INFORMATION THEFT COUNTERMEASURES

PART 8

SEMINARS

CONCLUSION

1. "U.S. Cost of Keeping Lid on Secrets is $2.7 Billion," *Chicago Tribune*, 1996.

BOOK ORDER FORM

BOOKS	Qty.	Amount
"Commercial Espionage: 79 Ways Competitors Can Get Any Business Secrets" U.S.D. $49.95		$
"Attorney's Work Product: Vital Legal Information Digest" U.S.D. $19.95		$
"How to Pass Exams On Any Subject" U.S.D. $39.95		$
SUBTOTAL		$
Illinois residents add 8.25% tax		$
Shipping and Handling: **$6.00** for the first book and **$2.00** for each additional book. For shipping to addresses outside the U.S.A., add **$30.00.**		$
TOTAL		$

ORDERED BY

Last Name: _____First Name: _____

Your Title (if applicable): _____

Name of organization/company : _____

Address: _____

City: _____State: _____Zip: _____Country: _____

Tel. : (   ) _____   Fax:: (   ) _____

ORDERING BY:

Phone   (have your credit card ready): **1-888-88-777-69** (within U.S.A.only)

Fax   (include your credit card info): **1-847-674-0759**

E-mail   **global@denvica-mall.com**

Mail   send a check, money order or bank's check payable to

Global Connection, Inc., or include your credit card information:

Global Connection, Inc.
P.O. Box 688
Skokie, IL 60076-0688

Payment   ☐ Check (issued by U.S.A. banks only) ☐ Money order ☐ Bank's check
☐ Credit Card: ☐ MasterCard ☐ AMEX ☐Visa ☐ Discover ☐ Optima
Card number: _____

Cardholder's Name:_____Exp. date:_____

• Delivery will be made to the cardholder's address only •

Visit our Internet site at **www.denvica-mall.com** to learn more about the above listed books.

Allow 4 to 6 weeks for delivery after receipt by Global Connection, Inc. of your order and the proper purchase amount. Defective book(s) will be replaced. You may return any book(s) in their original condition within 30 days for a complete refund. Prices are subject to change without notice.

DENVICA-MALL ONLINE
information emporium

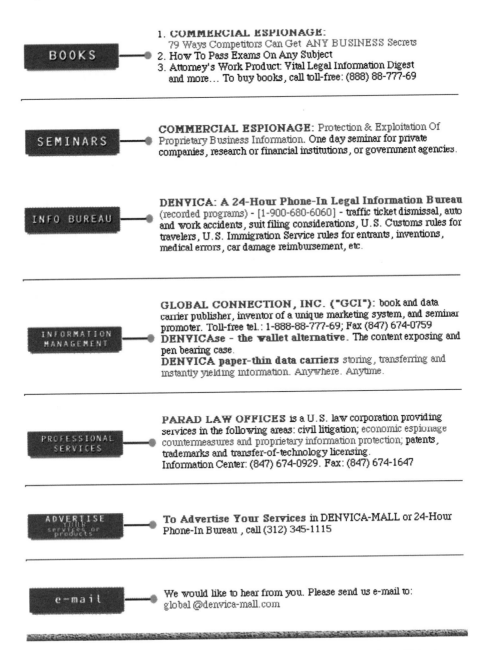

BOOKS

1. **COMMERCIAL ESPIONAGE:**
   79 Ways Competitors Can Get ANY BUSINESS Secrets
2. How To Pass Exams On Any Subject
3. Attorney's Work Product: Vital Legal Information Digest
   and more... To buy books, call toll-free: (888) 88-777-69

SEMINARS

COMMERCIAL ESPIONAGE: Protection & Exploitation Of Proprietary Business Information. One day seminar for private companies, research or financial institutions, or government agencies.

INFO BUREAU

DENVICA: A 24-Hour Phone-In Legal Information Bureau (recorded programs) - [1-900-680-6060] - traffic ticket dismissal, auto and work accidents, suit filing considerations, U.S. Customs rules for travelers, U.S. Immigration Service rules for entrants, inventions, medical errors, car damage reimbursement, etc.

INFORMATION MANAGEMENT

GLOBAL CONNECTION, INC. ("GCI"): book and data carrier publisher, inventor of a unique marketing system, and seminar promoter. Toll-free tel.: 1-888-88-777-69; Fax (847) 674-0759
DENVICAse - the wallet alternative. The content exposing and pen bearing case.
DENVICA paper-thin data carriers storing, transferring and instantly yielding information. Anywhere. Anytime.

PROFESSIONAL SERVICES

PARAD LAW OFFICES is a U.S. law corporation providing services in the following areas: civil litigation; economic espionage countermeasures and proprietary information protection; patents, trademarks and transfer-of-technology licensing.
Information Center: (847) 674-0929. Fax: (847) 674-1647

ADVERTISE YOUR services or products

To Advertise Your Services in DENVICA-MALL or 24-Hour Phone-In Bureau , call (312) 345-1115

e-mail

We would like to hear from you. Please send us e-mail to:
global @denvica-mall.com

Unique DENVICA® data carriers

The paper-thin carriers contain **personal** (telephones, document ID numbers, your address, etc.) **guiding** (driving directions, accident instructions) and **planning** (shopping list, daily schedules) data. Multicolor, business card size **carriers** are unique **individual** reminders, message carriers and records keepers. They increase their users' efficiency and productivity, prevent loss of valuable names and numbers and reveal data at a glance.

The write-on carriers are inexpensive, storable, wallet-kept and handy. They replace bulky daily planners, electronic "books" and throw-away notes. Carry-on tabbed carriers do what portable computers, "planner" notebooks, piles of scratch paper and mental notes cannot do, namely:

Driving Directions guide eliminates waste of time needed to find a scratch paper to jot down the address, identity of party/location and directions how to get to the respective destination. Unlike scratch paper, the carriers may be reused and stored for future reference. The directions are organized for hands-free following thereof while driving a car. (**Item A1**).

Shopping List is an organizer of items to be purchased. Simple. Convenient. Great for record keeping purposes. (**Item A2**).

Events is a quick reminder of important dates and events. The carrier assists in scheduling major occurrences during the year. (**Item A3**).

Planner is a general ledger for daily tasks (appointments, meetings, things to do, etc.). (**Item A4**).

Accident is an instruction form to be completed in case of an automobile accident.
It should be kept in a car. It will help to preserve the rights to recovery of damages arising from the accident. (**Item A5**).

Save money, time, efforts and records. Get lots of data write-on carriers for yourself, your friends, employees and clients.

DENVICA® CARRIERS' ORDER FORM

Item#	Description		Qty.	Amount
A1	Driving Directions (20 carrier package)	$5.00		$
A2	Shopping List (20 carrier package)	$5.00		$
A3	Events (20 carrier package)	$5.00		$
A4	Planner (20 carrier package)	$5.00		$
A5	Accident (20 carrier package)	$7.00		$
SUBTOTAL				$
Illinois residents add 8.25% tax				$
Shipping and Handling: **$8.95** (subtotal is $20-$200); **$14.95** (subtotal is $200-$500); **$20.95** (subtotal is $500-$800); **$24.95** (subtotal is over $800); For shipping to addresses outside the U.S.A., add **$30.00.**				$
TOTAL				$

ORDERED BY

Last Name: _____ First Name: _____

Your Title (if applicable): _____

Name of organization/company : _____

Address: _____

City: _____ State: _____ Zip: _____ Country: _____

Tel. : (   ) _____   Fax:: (   ) _____

ORDERING BY:

Phone (have your credit card ready): **1-888-88-777-69** (within U.S.A.only)

Fax (include your credit card info): **1-847-674-0759**

E-mail **global@denvica-mall.com**

Mail send a check, money order or bank's check payable to

Global Connection, Inc., or include your credit card information:

Global Connection, Inc.
P.O. Box 688
Skokie, IL 60076-0688

Payment ☐ Check (issued by U.S.A. banks only) ☐ Money order ☐ Bank's check
☐ Credit Card: ☐ MasterCard ☐ AMEX ☐Visa ☐ Discover ☐ Optima
Card number: _____

Cardholder's Name:_____Exp. date:_____

• Delivery will be made to the cardholder's address only •

Visit our Internet site at **www.denvica-mall.com** to learn more about the GCI products.

Allow 4 to 6 weeks for delivery after receipt by Global Connection, Inc. of your order and the proper purchase amount. Defective product(s) will be replaced. You may return any product(s) in their original condition within 30 days for a complete refund. Prices are subject to change without notice.